Helen Hunt Jackson

Helen Hunt Jackson

A Lonely Voice of Conscience

by Antoinette May

CHRONICLE BOOKS

Printed in the United States of America.

Library of Congress Cataloging-in-Publication Data

May, Antoinette.
  Helen Hunt Jackson: a lonely voice of conscience.
  Bibliography: p.
  Includes index.
  1. Jackson, Helen Maria Fiske Hunt, 1831-1885.
2. Authors, American—19th century—Biography.
3. West (U.S.) in literature. 4. Indians of North America in literature. I. Title.
PS2108.M39   1987   818'.409 [B]   87-6572
ISBN 0-87701-376-4 (pbk.)

Editing: Barbara Youngblood
Book and Cover Design: Linda Herman
Composition: Skillful Means Press

10 9 8 7 6 5 4 3 2 1

Chronicle Books
One Hallidie Plaza
San Francisco, CA 94102

For Charles Beardsley who provided the spark

Also by Antoinette May

Witness to War

Psychic Women

Different Drummers

Free Spirit

*Haunted Houses and Wandering Ghosts
of California*

Poems reprinted by permission of the publishers and the Trustees of Amherst College from *The Poems of Emily Dickinson,* edited by Thomas H. Johnson, Cambridge, Mass.: The Belknap Press of Harvard University Press, Copyright 1951, © 1955, 1979, 1983 by the President and Fellows of Harvard College.

Letters reprinted by permission of the publishers from *The Letters of Emily Dickinson,* Thomas H. Johnson, editor, Cambridge, Mass.: The Belknap Press of Harvard University Press, Copyright © 1958, 1986 by the President and Fellows of Harvard College.

Additional letters reprinted by permission of the Huntington Library, San Marino, California, and Special Collections, The Colorado College Library, Colorado Springs, Colorado.

Contents

Preface ix

Chapter One *Beginnings* 3

Chapter Two *Happy and Sad Times* 11

Chapter Three *Helen's Mentor* 22

Chapter Four *California Collage* 32

Chapter Five *A Fallen Angel* 39

Chapter Six *Helen of Colorado* 46

Chapter Seven *A Lawyer's Brief* 61

Chapter Eight *A Time Trip* 70

Chapter Nine *A Junketing Female Commissioner* 89

Chapter Ten *The Sugar Pill* 105

Chapter Eleven *Another Kind of Battle* 115

Chapter Twelve *Helen's Last Hurrah* 127

Chapter Thirteen *The Final Journey* 133

Bibliography 139

Index 143

Acknowledgments   This book owes its existence most directly to a special friend and mentor, John Wilson, whose editorial skill and creative instincts proved invaluable.

Another debt is to William S. Jackson Jr. and his wife, Patty, whose trust and generosity made this project possible.

Helen Hunt Jackson's writings — her books, poems, articles and, most importantly, her letters comprise the primary source for this book. It couldn't have been done without the assistance of the California Historical Society, the California State Library, The Huntington Library, the Pioneers' Museum, the San Diego Historical Society and — most specifically — Barbara Neilon and her staff at the Colorado College Library, Special Collections.

Finally, Larry Smith of Chronicle Books deserves special mention not only for commissioning the book in the first place but, by curious coincidence, signing it into being in his San Francisco office on August 12, 1985 — one hundred years to the day of Helen Hunt Jackson's death in that same city.

Preface

Some people just don't give up, and Helen Hunt Jackson was one of them.

For her, writing took the place of living when at thirty-four she had — by accident or illness — lost husband, children, parents. With a survivor's instincts, she sought out the best mentor in the country, then quickly surpassed him. A child of her times, she sensed almost immediately what people wanted to read and soon acquired the skill to give it to them. At first a poet, she easily mastered the techniques necessary to write essays, travel articles, short stories, and finally novels.

Her success was critical as well as popular. Ralph Waldo Emerson, when asked if he didn't think Helen Hunt Jackson the best woman poet on the continent, replied, "Perhaps we might as well omit woman." It was said that he clipped her poems from newspapers so that he could carry them about with him to read aloud.

Passionate, daring, defiant, a woman who lived by her own rules, moving as freely in an age of stagecoaches and steamships as jet-setters do today, Helen lived a life that few women of her day had the courage to live. In any era she would qualify as truly original.

Married finally to William Jackson, a financier and railroad magnate considered the best catch in the Colorado Territory and six years younger than she, Helen appeared to have it all. Approaching fifty and a gifted writer, however, she was still seeking a purpose. Then a chance encounter with two beleaguered American Indians. In the past she'd been too busy leading her own life, pursuing her own varied goals, to be even remotely interested in crusading for someone else's. Now suddenly the pathos of the situation, the direct appeal of individuals in need, had the force of a religious conversion. The result would make political and literary history and forever change the course of Helen's life. Finding her purpose, she was consumed and, in the process, accomplished her greatest work.

In 1881 Helen Hunt Jackson declared war on the U.S. government with the publication of *A Century of Dishonor,* a scathing indictment of federal Indian policy. When Congress convened that year, each member found a copy of the book on his desk. When reaction proved underwhelming, she engaged in a paper duel with Secretary of the Interior Carl Schurz. The result of Helen's barrage of petitions, tracts, and newspaper articles was her appointment as special commissioner to study the conditions of the Indians.

It was a landmark decision. She was the first woman to hold that position, but once again the results were disappointing. Helen's report was virtually ignored. If the country was to get her message — and heed it — a sweetener was needed. She determined to provide it. *Ramona* was written at white heat from a sense of moral outrage at the manner in which the government had robbed the Indians of their lands. It vividly portrays three cultures — Indian, Mexican, and Anglo — locked in combat; only one could survive. What on the surface appears to be a tender romance is actually a bitter indictment of the American doctrine of manifest destiny.

She wrote with elegance and feeling, her independence adding zest to her opinions. If at times her characters appear idealized by today's standards, they are nonetheless *real. Ramona* works today as it did in 1884. Its protagonists come vividly to life, fulfilling themselves as real men and women. Characters collide, sparks fly, tears flow. The reader is swept along to the last page of the curiously unhappy ending.

Small wonder the novel has been reprinted more than three hundred times; translated widely; made into three movies, countless plays, and an annual pageant; and lent its name to a song, streets, schools, towns, and even a convent.

Her purpose was to right a wrong; the creation of an enduring piece of fiction was secondary. As the *Uncle Tom's Cabin* of the southwestern Indians, *Ramona* was the first California protest novel, its author the first woman to take a political stance in favor of the Indian — all the more remarkable in an era when many people believed "the only good Indian is a dead one." Initial reviews were indifferent. *Ramona* gained recognition on its own power, reaching such a degree of popularity that it was acclaimed some thirty years later as the great American novel. Even today the docudrama remains the classic novel of Southern California.

The power and passion of Helen Hunt Jackson moved hundreds of thousands of readers. *Ramona* is more than a historical novel — it is history, and she with it.

Helen Hunt Jackson

CHAPTER ONE

Beginnings

All her life Helen Hunt Jackson would say one thing, then turn around and do something else entirely. That one of the great social activists of the nineteenth century should be openly disdainful of "cause women" wouldn't have surprised anyone who knew her.

Nonconformist, inconsistent, Helen was from beginning to end a law unto herself. Those closest to her could agree on one thing only: she was "the most brilliant, impetuous and thoroughly independent woman of her time."

Helen's parents, Nathan Wiley and Deborah (Vinal) Fiske, were New Englanders who took their Puritan heritage to heart. When their firstborn died in infancy, they bore up bravely. "The Lord hath given and the Lord hath taken away," Nathan, a Congregational clergyman and a professor of philosophy and language at Amherst College intoned. "We feel it to be the fatherly chastisement that we need," Deborah dutifully agreed.

"I inherited nothing from either of my parents except my mother's gift for cheer," Helen was to say more than once. She was indeed a strange fledgling for such a nest. A born radical, impulsive, eager for experience, determined to accept nothing that she herself hadn't tested, Helen was as disturbing and provocative as a tropical bird among austere wrens.

The Fiskes had hoped for another son, but it was Helen Maria who was born on October 14, 1830.

Unlike the two children who followed — Heman Humphrey, who died in infancy, and Ann — she was a problem. "I cannot play with Helen so well as with Ann," their mother admitted. "Helen is so wild — jumping rope, dressing up in odd things, jumping out behind doors. . . . Ann does not require the vigilance Helen does. She is honest, artless, and affectionate — telling the whole of everything *right out,* and everybody how well she loves them, while Miss Helen has no idea of 'liking all those folks' nor of telling the whole of everything. Helen has the most *downright* frolics, but Ann is happiest. They are as unlike, as Papa often says, 'as if they belonged to different nations.'"Impulsive, selective, private — Helen as she was then and as she would always be.

Gentle Deborah shared some of her husband's disapproval of Papa Vinal — her father — a successful contractor who enjoyed his brandy. Vinal never attempted to hide his liking for money and the things it would buy. Honest but shrewd, he could drive a hard bargain, a trait his granddaughter would inherit. "Help Papa become pious," Deborah had often prayed, and now she added a plea for her daughter as well.

A charmer like her worldly grandfather, Helen was also audacious and independent. At six the wanderlust that motivated much of her life first manifested itself. While picking berries in the forest behind her home, Helen, swept away by desire for adventure, persuaded a neighbor child to go exploring with her. "We'll see live snails with horns," she promised. Happily they wandered through the forest while the whole town searched for them. When two Amherst professors finally spotted the girls, they'd walked four miles, pausing to rest at a funeral in a nearby town.

Helen hated being caught: there was still so much left to see and do. Unwilling to be returned so soon to the confines of home, she jumped from the carriage, only to be captured and delivered to her doorstep. Deborah, at the close of that remarkable day, recorded her daughter's homecoming in a journal: "Helen walked in a quarter before ten o'clock at night, as rosy and smiling as possible, and saying in her brightest tone, 'Oh, Mother! I've had a perfectly splendid time.'"

Neither parent was amused, and when a few days passed with no sign of remorse, Nathan banished her to the attic. The forced inactivity was too much for Helen, and before long she had discovered a nail and was driving holes in the plaster. Furious, Nathan administered a severe whipping and continued the confinement for a whole week. Helen carried the memory always— that one and others; and some forty years later was still bitter enough to admit, "I myself was whipped . . . but I never lacked anything but the power to kill every human being who struck me."

It couldn't have been easy for Nathan, with his uncompromising Calvinist ways, to understand Helen's high spirits, and his stern attitudes were an even greater enigma to her. Once when she was sent to the study to find a book for him, she mistakenly returned with the wrong one and was called stupid for her trouble. She could never forget the experience of being humiliated before strangers by her own father.

Though descended from clergymen and missionaries, Helen must have missed her father's sermon on turning the other cheek, a virtue that would never be hers. Helen had her own priorities; a passionate loyalty was one. Her cat Midge was an early example. A seeming wonder cat who followed her to school and once even to a funeral, Midge was as much a friend and confidant as a pet. The kinship went even deeper because of Midge's history. Years earlier the old tom had fallen into a barrel of soft soap, badly scalding himself before Grandpa Vinal had managed to fish him out. Knowing how much Midge meant to Helen, Vinal had ordered the cradle brought down from the attic, tucked the frightened cat tenderly inside, and soothed it with warm milk laced with his best brandy. Despite his applying hair restorer to the bare spots where Midge's hair had fallen out, the cat remained semihairless and an invalid with one blind eye.

Then one day — in a fit of misguided sympathy, thinking the cat would be better off dead — Cousin Josiah Stearns, who lived with the Fiskes while attending college, took it upon himself to drown Midge in a nearby pond. Helen was distraught and then furious. She vowed never to speak to her cousin again. When she descended the stairs the next morning, Helen's whole body quivered as she shook her fist at the young man so much taller than she was. "I said I'd never speak to you as long as I live, but I will one more time," she announced. "You're a murderer, that's what you are! And when you get to be a missionary, I hope the cannibals will eat you."

It was Nathan's turn to be furious. In nineteenth-century New England the direct expression of anger was not to be tolerated in women or children. He demanded that his daughter apologize. Eventually Helen complied, but it was obvious to everyone that she didn't mean a word of it.

Grownups simply didn't understand, and Annie was still such a little girl. Helen was fortunate therefore to have one close friend to whom she could tell her troubles. Just down the street lived Emily Dickinson, only two months younger than Helen and destined to be a lifelong friend. Tiny, frail Emily, with her soft voice and shy, diffident manner, was outwardly as different from the chubby, bubbly Helen as two girls could be. Beneath the deceptive surface, however, she was much like her: bright, impish, fanciful. Both loved to hide behind the syringa bushes, eluding the adults while regaling each other with secrets, imagined adventures, and ghost stories.

Helen needed a happy respite from the sadness that was beginning to pervade the Fiske household. Deborah wasn't well. Each day she slipped a little farther into the shadows. Helen tried desperately to please. She adored her mother, but chafed at any restraint. Lessons were particularly arduous. While Ann learned slowly, puzzling over each word, Helen leaped ahead, sometimes skipping words she didn't know or replacing them with substitutes that *seemed* right. Deborah often despaired of teaching her. "Helen learns very well," she wrote, "but I do not drive her very much to make her very literary — she is quite inclined to question the author of everything; the Bible, she says, does not feel as if it were true. . . ."

Poor Calvinist mother, perhaps realizing that her own soul wasn't long for this world, she worried all the more about Helen's. When Deborah grew too weak to see to Helen's education, the recalcitrant nine-year-old joined her friend Emily at Amherst Academy, a public school, even though both parents feared it wasn't strict enough for her.

Helen was only a few months past her twelfth birthday when, in 1844, Deborah died of tuberculosis and the sisters were separated. Ann was sent to live with relatives, Helen to a series of seminaries. From that time they would see one another only on holidays and later on occasional visits as married women.

Nathan, also suffering from tuberculosis, ended his twenty-two-year career at Amherst College in the summer of 1846. The institution, founded by Samuel Dickinson, Emily's grandfather, as a religious stronghold for the defense and promulgation of the faith, had suited him well. Now he had but one wish — to visit the Holy Land. After carefully collecting all of Deborah's letters and other mementoes and entrusting them to Helen and Ann, he set off in late September. In May of the following year, he was buried on Mount Zion.

With both parents gone and her sister far away, Helen was alone and adrift, a bird of passage. The wanderings that would characterize her entire life had begun. Moving from school to school, her vacations divided between a variety of relatives, she thought wistfully of the familiarity and continuity of Amherst and delighted in Emily's correspondence.

Emily poured out her heart in long letters written by candlelight long after the rest of the Dickinsons had retired. Helen was not so faithful. "My prodigal H.," Emily called her — she could scarcely understand a life so full of movement and change. Despite her bouts of loneliness, Helen's memory of "home" was receding. Slowly, imperceptibly, she was beginning to reach out to the world.

In 1848 a tea caddy of nuggets was presented to President Polk, glittering evidence of gold in California, the romantic and mysterious far-western colony that had only recently become a state. Helen, attending the Abbott Institute in New York, a select boarding school maintained by family friends, was excited by the vivid accounts that enlivened the newspapers. Almost all editions carried long lists of boats headed for the Gold Country. Ships were departing daily, some going around the Horn and others headed for Nicaragua, where intrepid gold seekers traveled across the isthmus jungle by mules and wagons. On the western side they boarded another ship, which took them up the coast to San Francisco.

Helen avidly scanned the "Ho, California" column that appeared each day in the *New York Herald*. More and more Californians were exchanging gold for goods to take or send back by steamer. Helen was fascinated by their stories and resolved to one day see for herself this exciting new land.

In the meantime she contented herself with school, shopping, sightseeing, and parties — many parties. Looking back at this period after many years, a friend attempted to describe Helen, "not exactly beautiful," yet "gracious and vivacious." Most remarkable were her eyes, which Helen called "green" and which were "more alive" than any her friend had ever known.

These were the "best and brightest" of Helen's school days, a time when her natural brilliance and enthusiasm finally found focus. The Abbott Institute suited her perfectly. She thrived in an atmosphere where rules were minimal and students self-disciplined. Almost without realizing it, Helen earned the reputation of a scholar and, upon graduation, was pleased and flattered to be invited to join the staff as a teacher. She accepted eagerly, and the months seemed to fly by. "New York is my Arcadia," she wrote to a former roommate. "I need not tell you that I am perfectly happy. Teaching I enjoy most highly — so much that I can truly say, I was never so happy in my life as at this time."

So she wasn't pleased when the letter arrived. It wasn't bad enough that the school term was ending, but here was vacation beginning again with a visit to yet another set of family friends. She was to summer with the Reverend Ray Palmer, pastor of the first Congregational Church in Albany, and his family.

How dreary! Helen had had enough of prayers and long faces. Besides, she loved the excitement and bustle of New York, the challenge of her new job. The thought of languishing for an entire summer at the home of a provincial clergyman was too much to be borne. But of course she had to bear it. Grandpa Vinal had made his wishes very clear. Shortly after Nathan's death, he'd drawn up his will in favor of his two orphaned granddaughters and named Deacon Julius Palmer of Boston the executor, trustee and coguardian. Some of those duties were shared in some measure by Deacon Palmer's brother, the Reverend Ray Palmer. In no way could Helen appear to slight him.

The day came when school was over, her bags packed, all arrangements made. Jennie Abbott drove her to the railroad station, and the two young women talked enthusiastically about the fall term. Forcing a cheerful smile, Helen waved animatedly from the window, then settled back among the assorted hatboxes, parcels, and carpetbags that surrounded her. The train began to move.

Albany wasn't where she wanted to be, but at least it was some place she had not been. As always, Helen's spirits brightened at the prospect of an adventure. Albany was the state capital and just might be interesting. At least there would be a few parties, new people. No doubt the time would pass quickly enough. Three months wasn't so *awfully* long.

What Helen expected was a summer's diversion. What awaited her was love.

CHAPTER TWO

Happy and Sad Times

Lieutenant Edward Bissel Hunt wasn't much for grand balls. But what could he do when the state governor who hosted the affair was his very own brother?

Both bright and enterprising — he had graduated second in his West Point class — Hunt probably knew that he was considered an excellent catch. Possibly that's why, despite his rugged good looks, impressive career potential, and excellent social connections, he'd managed to reach thirty without serious entanglement.

On the night of August 9, 1851, his mind was very much on air — or at least its use in conveying mechanical power — for that was the subject of the paper he was to deliver at the sixth annual meeting of the American Association for the Advancement of Science. Possessed of a scientist's single-mindedness, he may not have been aware of just how handsome he looked in his dark blue dress uniform worn with a scarlet military cape and dress sword.

But Helen noticed and was drawn immediately to the tall, dark stranger. Since her arrival in Albany a few weeks earlier, her success with the locals had been dazzling. As an acknowledged belle, she looked with interest at this attractive newcomer.

Helen was more than beautiful. An elegant ash blond, her voluptuous figure was set off to perfection by the fashions of the day — bodices that fit like they'd been pasted on and skirts that flared just enough to emphasize a tiny waistline without being too full for graceful movement. The appreciation of elegance that had surfaced early despite her parents' bleak conservatism had matured into a fine sense of style that would always distinguish her. Fortunately Grandpa Vinal saw nothing wrong with a girl looking pretty and had the wherewithal to indulge her.

Headstrong, brilliant, and vivacious, Helen was used to commanding center stage at social gatherings. Her tiny feet and exquisite hands with their long tapering fingers were much admired; and now, head thrown back, blue-green eyes sparkling mischievously, she was aware that her physical assets were much in evidence as she whirled past him.

Edward had progressed to his present high-ranking position in the Coast Survey — then a subdivision of the Treasury Department — by determining exactly what he wanted then proceeding unwaveringly in that direction. During the intermission he moved without hesitation to a place beside Helen, and from then on they danced every dance together. In the days that followed, as often as he could absent himself from his temporary assignment in New York City, he joined the young men who overflowed the Palmer parsonage — but with a difference. Helen had enjoyed the reputation of a "demure flirt." After so many years of discipline and often loneliness, she thrived on the attention and gaiety in Albany. Now at last her heart had come out of exile.

Fall came and went and with it the teaching position at the Abbott Institute. Helen remained with the Palmers — a family she'd come to love — eagerly anticipating Edward's visits and hoping for a proposal. It didn't come. She waited and worried. Was she too young for him? Too frivolous, perhaps?

In April the Julius Palmers, her coguardians, planned a two-month trip to St. Louis and invited her to accompany them. Helen hesitated. The waiting was getting on her nerves. Perhaps absence really did make the heart grow fonder ... and if it didn't, wasn't it time she got on with her life?

She accepted.

To her delight, the first person Helen saw as she boarded the overnight steamer for New York was Edward. Then another admirer, Charles Clark, appeared. Surely it did no harm for Edward to see this evidence of Clark's interest. What Helen didn't want, however, was another person hanging around just when Edward might propose. Fortunately Charles had merely come to "wish her well and bid her goodbye."

During their stop in New York, Edward took her to the government lithographing rooms to show her the charts he'd engraved. Excited by being back in the big city, Helen took him to her favorite haunts: Union Square and Fifth Avenue. Later that day he accompanied her party on the next leg of the journey, taking the two o'clock boat to South Amboy, New Jersey, before returning to his home base in Washington, D.C.

When Helen reached Baltimore a few days later, a letter was waiting. It contained a miniature of Edward and his proposal. Excitedly she penned a letter to Mrs. Ray Palmer, who had become a kind of big sister— mother, "I know now the depth of his interest in me and have not one cloud of anxiety for the future." Still there was a cautious footnote: "Don't breathe ... a syllable outside the privacy of home circle at 157, not even to Mrs. Wood. . . ."

A few days later, still en route to St. Louis, she was reunited with Hunt in Washington. This time Helen felt sufficiently confident to write, "You may make things without reserve — I am wholly, wholly happy!" She even suggested that if Mother Palmer's expected baby was a boy that she name it Edward.

The rigid formalities of the day required a written acceptance to a marriage proposal. Helen's guardian insisted upon including a note of his own. It, like Deacon Palmer himself, was "characteristic constitutional, immovable and irresistible *prudence*." Helen didn't like it at all and complained to Palmer's daughter: "Such an arrangement is all right, I suppose, but hardly to my taste. Your father's prudence has made me look cautious and reserved." But for once she was too happy to rebel, and when she finally reached St. Louis, Helen forwarded his letter along with her own.

While part of her responded as always to the adventure of new places and people, she was becoming impatient with the delays imposed by the trip. In a note to Mrs. Palmer, she tried to explain her conflicting emotions: "Not that I do not want to take this journey. I want to go — very, very much. I think very likely it will be the last opportunity I shall have for many years of taking a long journey, but I *cannot* help wishing it were over."

By June Helen was back in Albany, but soon off to Boston for trousseau shopping with Ann. Occasionally Edward was able to get away for a visit. On one of those occasions, he was spotted by Austin Dickinson, Emily's younger brother, who wrote a surprisingly derogatory description to his fiancée, Susan Gilbert: "I was perched on top of an omnibus and she was on the walk with a large ambling, longfaced, ungraceful brassbuttoned individual of some forty or fifty years, I should judge, whom from his manner I took to be her lieutenant." Austin then speculated on "the probable bliss of them as a couple."

Occasionally Helen wondered, too, though her own appraisal was far more flattering than Austin's. Possibly it was their very differences that brought them closer. Edward was older — though not so old as Austin's absurdly catty estimate — much more serious than she, and very dedicated to his work. Helen perceived him as an anchor, as someone she could rely upon, but still she wished that there was more opportunity for them to spend time together before the wedding. Sometimes she felt overwhelmed by the enormity of it all and feared that they would come together as strangers.

As the date of her nuptials rushed toward her, Helen grew curiously nostalgic and introspective. One day while visiting in Amherst, she chanced to walk past her childhood home. Looking into the garden, she saw a "baby wagon" and was certain that it was the very one that had been used to pull her and Annie. In a letter to Mrs. Palmer, she speculated that it "had been left behind as a worthless piece of lumber for it was terribly dilapidated."

Helen felt the passage of time very keenly, commenting: "There I stood twenty-two, a world wanderer about to assume all the burdens of life and there was the wagon and the garden in all through which so little while since I was drawn by a young mother! It is a queer thing this life — isn't it? Thirty years from now very likely I shall have been as long silent as my mother has and my daughter may be speculating on the quick changes in the world."

In 1852, on the 28th day of October, Helen and Edward were married at Mount Vernon Church in Boston. Attended by Ann, Helen went to the altar wearing a pale blue taffeta gown. She'd selected blue remembering it had been her choice the night of the governor's ball. She hoped it would bring her luck. They were a striking couple. At five feet three inches, the bride barely reached to her husband's shoulder. He was as dark as she was fair.

If Helen felt misgivings at her bridegroom's sudden attack of "bilious dyspepsia," it isn't recorded. The honeymoon trip to Niagara Falls was postponed, and the couple stayed instead for a few days in Albany with the Palmers — not a very happy place, for the new baby, whom Helen would have named Edward, had sickened suddenly and died. The bridegroom recovered; they went on to visit his relatives in upper New York, where a sudden snowstorm canceled their trip to the falls. "Fortunately," Edward wrote the Palmers, "we find our climate in the head and it is summer here."

Helen tried to be philosophical. "Just imagine a bridal couple, standing under an umbrella with their teeth chattering and their feet wet to look at the Falls. It would be ludicrous." But she had to admit to Mrs. Palmer that Hunt's Hollow was "one of the wildest places you can imagine, small, countrified and lonely." She hoped to get away "without mortifying Edward or offending the natives."

By November 12 they had moved to Washington and were settled into their first home — rooms in Mrs. Reed's boardinghouse on F Street. Helen described Washington as "the city of politicians," but being a city of fashion as well, it suited her. As an officer's wife, she was expected to attend a constant round of social activities. Fortunately ten years of assorted boarding schools and continual residence in other people's homes had taught her the fine art of adjustment. Smiling inwardly at a commanding officer so little aware of literature that he thought Hawthorne's *Snow Image* a child's fairy tale, the highly intellectual Helen simply "adapted her conversation to a gentlemanly blockhead."

Helen loved controversy — she always had — and it was hard to avoid defending Harriet Beecher Stowe when she heard the author of *Uncle Tom's Cabin* called "a talented fiend in human shape." Helen enjoyed a rousing discussion, but Edward, a staunch conservative, mistrusted abolitionists and feared his wife "was a little infected." The loving bride held her tongue, wanting nothing more than to please him. Helen had become a highly social woman, a marvelous asset to an officer on his way up.

In June Edward was ordered to report back to the engineering office in New York City for summer duty. It was the first of many separations occasioned by his work and happened when Helen was least ready for it. In the last months of pregnancy, she had been advised not to travel. It was a lonely time, but the reward came in September when Murray Hunt was born. Edward wrote delightedly to the Ray Palmers, "He has blue eyes and knows how to cry already."

For the new mother the weeks seemed to fly. "Poor nineteenth century — on its last fifty!" she philosophized to "Mother" Palmer on January 2, 1854. "And in a little while — with all its fashion and improvements and self satisfactions it will all be laughed at as an 'olden time' and *we too* with it. Alas — we can't help it, do what we may! Is it not provoking to imagine some particularly choice dress or some pet hat of ours (one from Mrs. Blanchard's, say) dragged to light in 1946 . . . to amuse callers with when conversation runs low?"

Then Helen hastened to assure her friend that she wasn't tipsy on New Year's cheer, had had as a matter of fact only a half glass of apple toddy the day before when she and Edward had accompanied the Preston Blairs — who lived in what is now called Blair House — in making calls on Washington dignitaries.

Surely the most noteworthy call had been made upon Mrs. Alexander Hamilton, widow of the Federalist patriot, who was then ninety-six. Helen thought the visit eerie and dismal, "like hearing Ecclesiastes read in the middle of a forest." Mrs. Hamilton was "very old, so feeble, so much another world that it seemed almost a mockery to have her bear any part in the ceremonies of the day. She is very deaf and could not stand to welcome her callers but had a daughter with her to lead them up one by one and introduce them. She is the most ancient woman in the country and this gives her a peculiar interest but I should hate to live so long that people would come to see me as they would go to a relic. It would seem like being some sort of live *mummy*!"

The grim specter of Mrs. Hamilton haunted Helen, seeming to presage tragedy. Three months later her beloved grandfather died, the shrewd, loving friend who'd been far more a father to her than her own. Then in August an even greater loss: Murray, less than a year old, was dead of "dropsy of the brain."

A year later a second son, Warren Horsford Hunt — named for two of Edward's closest friends, but called Rennie by Helen — was born. Her pregnancy had been marred by inexplicable doubts, of which she had written a friend: "I could talk a long while with you about the strange mixture of longing and fear with which I *wait*: — how I almost dread to find again my whole soul so utterly bound up in one little frail life! — You know me well enough to know that I can't love after any *half way* fashion — but you can probably form a little idea of the painful intensity of how my love for a child — in spite of the exquisite delight, *saddens* every moment of my consciousness." But holding Rennie, she forgot the fears that had plagued her and thought only of the happiness of the moment. "They were intimate friends when he was little more than a baby," a friend would later recall, describing the closeness between mother and son as "the best and happiest" she had ever seen.

"She was gay, pleasure-loving, impulsive to the point of rashness in speech and action, never able to comprehend that word or act of hers could provoke unkind comment or misconstruction," her friend recalled years later, adding, "but she was so fresh, so warmhearted, so entertaining, that no one who knew her well could help loving her."

Helen found herself immersed in the women's world of the officer's wife, balanced precariously between being the authoritative decision maker in her husband's absence and the subservient "little woman" when he was at home. It was a life of coping and adapting, brightened immeasurably by Rennie's companionship. She followed Edward whenever possible, but often his assignments took him to places where she couldn't go.

And when her husband was at home, his mind was very often on other things. "If Edward seems preoccupied," his wife explained to a friend, "he is probably planning his work. Work, either with his head or hands, is an absolute necessity for him. Often he loses track of time and may even spend the whole night on his studies without going to bed."

Hunt's brilliant tract on molecular theory, *Nature of Forces,* had won him instant recognition; and he was considered one of the most promising physicists in the country. As the years passed, he wrote extensively for the *American Journal of Science* and continued to prepare papers for the American Association for the Advancement of Science.

Following one presentation in Newport, Helen persuaded him to accompany her and six-year-old Rennie to Amherst for commencement week. The highlight for her was a reception given by Emily Dickinson's parents on August 8, 1860. Helen and Emily had played together in that house when they were younger than Rennie. Now both were nearly thirty. Helen looked searchingly at her old friend and found the lively, whimsical playmate much changed. Where she herself had grown more worldly, Emily had pulled back, withdrawing farther and farther into a self-imposed shell. People told strange tales of Emily, such as how she ran from the room at the sound of the doorbell and hid herself when old friends came to call. But today Helen found her all wit and sparkle, brown eyes touched with the rich highlights she remembered from childhood.

Edward thought her a bit too witty for his taste. Later he would remember Emily as "uncanny." He was bewildered by this somewhat kittenish spinster with her high, breathless voice and smooth reddish braids pulled primly back into a bun. Unlike his own Helen, who was all candor and bright impetuosity, Emily's conversation consisted mostly of confusing epigrams. Still, she was his wife's friend, and Edward determined to do his best. When Carlo, Emily's large, shaggy dog, cleverly rubbed himself against the leg of the food-laden table until a piece of cake fell into his open mouth, Edward congratulated her on having a dog that understood gravity. Challenged by her ambiguity, he ventured a little of his own, "I will come again in a year," he promised, adding, "If I stay a shorter time it will be longer." Ten years later Emily would confide to an admirer of Helen's that Major Hunt interested her more than any man she'd ever met.

Within a year the South had seceded, war was declared, and Edward was dispatched to Key West to defend Fort Taylor. Successful in saving it for the Union despite strong Southern opposition, he was ordered to Virginia as chief officer in the Shenandoah campaign. Helen busied herself with volunteer work at a military hospital, but found her services more in demand as a mender and reader than as a nurse.

Then came the news. Edward was being sent north to test his newest invention, "the sea-miner"—a submarine gun. Helen set up housekeeping in New York while Edward continued his experiments at the Brooklyn Navy Yard. If successful, his creation—a prototype of the modern torpedo—would revolutionize naval warfare.

A partially submerged watertight hull was constructed, from which a projectile was to be fired. The fumes were supposed to be expelled through an aperture on the top surface of the hull. The trial run was held September 30. Confidently descending from the aperture by means of a ladder, Edward reached the bottom of the hull, where he found the chamber filled with deadly gas, which someone had forgotten to drain. Turning quickly, he attempted to climb the ladder, but fell to the bottom, striking his head. Several men who tried to rescue him were also overcome. All were resuscitated but Edward, who suffered from concussion. He died October 2, 1863, just three weeks short of his eleventh wedding anniversary.

Much later Helen's reactions to the tragedy would be attributed to Draxy in the story "The Elder's Wife," who, like herself, shed no tears, choosing instead to shut herself away from her friends until her self-control was restored. Determined to be cheerful for her child's sake and unwilling to be parted from him, Draxy established a school to teach him and his friends. While Draxy's—and Helen's—wifehood had been "lovely, intense," motherhood was greater. Draxy's only fear was the depth and single-mindedness of her love for her child. And that was Helen's as well.

Just eighteen months after the death of his father, Rennie contracted diphtheria. He and Helen had been vacationing with Ann, who was now married and pregnant with her fifth child. When two of Ann's children as well as Rennie became ill, Helen attempted to nurse them all, but soon became seriously ill herself.

Though only nine years old, Rennie reacted with amazing tenderness, courage, and perception. Helen had always found it difficult to reprimand him and could never insist that he obey her without first giving him a careful explanation of why the act was necessary. Now he showed the same affection and understanding of her. Realizing that he was dying, the child pleaded, "Promise me, Mama, that you won't kill yourself."

· Helen exacted from him in return a pledge that if it were possible he would come back and talk with her from the other world. After Rennie's death on April 13, 1865, Helen lay awake night after night praying that he would appear to her. Spiritualism was popular, and there were numerous wonder tales, but nothing happened to her. Helen's faith waned. At last she decided that what Rennie couldn't do simply wasn't possible. Still, there was always the hope, and a thread of the supernatural wove its way through many of her books.

And so a second son was buried at West Point, beside his father and brother. "And I alone," she grieved, "am left, who avail nothing." For months after Rennie's death, Helen shut herself away from friends and family; and when she appeared among them at last, she was smiling, vivacious, outwardly unchanged.

CHAPTER THREE

Helen's Mentor

At thirty-five Helen was at the height of her physical appeal. The heavy mourning she'd adopted merely added an air of piquancy to her voluptuous figure and vivid coloring. The daughter of an Amherst professor, she'd grown up among intellectuals; and as the wife of a brilliant army officer and the sister-in-law of the governor of New York, she'd traveled in distinguished society. The self-assurance acquired in those circles, coupled with her natural audacity, gave Helen a flair that few could equal.

She was starting over, beginning a new life, and had chosen her setting carefully. She would write. Not merely letters: all women in her circle were adept at that, cultivating early the skill of penning stylish little notes just as they'd learned to paint china or play the piano — not well necessarily, but pleasingly. Such entertainments were encouraged as prenuptial busywork, and if a woman didn't have too many children, she could go on entertaining herself as a letter writer indefinitely. A few even indulged themselves with journals. Helen had never had much time for that, but in the months that followed Rennie's death she began to write poetry.

Out of the depths of her grief had come "The Key to the Casket," written just six weeks after her loss. On an impulse she signed the poem Marah — a play on "Ma of Rennie Hunt" — and sent it off to Parke Godwin, assistant publisher of the *New York Evening Post*. Its appearance on June 9, 1865, was a beginning. There were other Marah poems, the best known, "Lifted Over," bringing encouragement and recognition as other bereaved mothers responded with warm notes. She liked the thought that words of hers had brought comfort to others. Then as variations of her work began to appear, Helen realized that she was actually being imitated.

The flattery raised her spirits immeasurably. She was inspired to travel once again, and her New England rambles were recorded in a prose piece — her first — that Godwin also printed. It was her first actual sale and the first money she had ever earned. She decided to forsake the pseudonym Marah — its connotations were too sorrowful — substituting the initials H. H. Helen Hunt was too alliterative, like "Fannie Fern" or "Minnie Myrtle," sugary pen names she disdained. Additionally, she was well aware that readers were frequently hostile to women writers, calling them "ink-stained women" and refusing to take them seriously.

Helen was very serious about her writing and ready to do something about it. The place from which to launch herself was indisputably Newport, Rhode Island, a select seaport city where writing had become a lifestyle. Reputed to have more authors than any other city in the country, its king was Thomas Wentworth Higginson.

She'd met Colonel Higginson briefly ten years earlier at a scientific gathering and had followed his career. There was much to follow. Beginning as a clergyman, Higginson's consistently liberal views had cost him his pulpit. He'd conspired openly with John Brown, aided fugitive slaves, and ridden into politically torn Kansas during the bloody fifties with a money belt stuffed with funds for the Free State forces and a rifle to defend it. Later he recruited a regiment for the Civil War, but resigned as its colonel to take command of the first formally organized regiment of freed slaves.

Although controversy always stimulated Helen, what drew her like a magnet to Higginson was his outspoken advocacy of economic equality for women. Helen wanted income as well as solace from her work. For years she'd admired his articles in *Atlantic Monthly*; then one in particular, "A letter to a Young Contributor," caught her eye. It discussed everything from the art of writing to methods of getting an editor's attention. An essayist, a reformer, a friend of everyone who was anyone — wasn't Higginson the very one to advise her?

Hannah Dame's boardinghouse was *the* place to stay in Newport. Colonel Higginson himself presided at the family table in the dining room, carving for as many as forty people on special occasions. Later he would describe Helen as a woman "whose very temperament seemed mingled of sunshine and fire," but on the evening of her arrival — February 10, 1866 — his journal contained only the hope that despite her deep mourning, "which bespoke a private depression, her so-far invariable high spirits might prove her an acquisition" to their intellectual commune.

The years had had little effect upon Thomas Higginson. He was the same handsome, vigorous man that Helen remembered, quick yet tactful, a mocking gentleness about the eyes and mouth. But now there was a look of hidden sadness, a sense of quiet resignation that touched her. Helen quickly discovered the cause: Higginson's wife, Mary, found her passion in dependency. Mary's affection was for her illness, a mysterious affliction that kept her confined to a wheelchair. She would admit few people to their rooms and rarely accompanied her husband on outings, even though he'd designed a special cab that made it possible for him to wheel her directly into their carriage.

Small wonder the quality that first impressed Higginson about Helen was her cheerfulness. Whatever private devils may have plagued her, she appeared high spirited and vital in the presence of others. Invited to small gatherings in the two rooms assigned her, he found them transformed by Japanese prints, cherished family silver, flowers and oriental hangings. Like Helen herself, the place was warm and inviting, an oasis promising excitement as well as peace.

Newport, the self-styled literary capital of America, considered itself avant-garde, but even there Helen was thought "modern," a sophisticated woman of the world whose presence livened any gathering. Higginson saw to it that she met everybody worth knowing, including Ralph Waldo Emerson and Julia Ward Howe, whose "Battle Hymn of the Republic" had made her a Newport star; but he managed time alone with her as well. There were evenings at the theater — once he took her all the way to Boston to hear Charles Dickens read from his own works — and days of horseback riding and sailing.

Within a month Helen had shown him a few of her verses and asked for advice. Higginson knew another aspiring writer from Amherst. "Have you met Emily Dickinson?" he asked and confided that Emily had written to him shortly after the publication of his literary advice artice. When he told Helen that Emily's letters had pursued him from post to post during the war, she could almost hear her friend's naively hesitant voice floating into that martial atmosphere: "Mr. Higginson, are you too deeply occupied to say if my verse is alive?" And later to the Port Royal front, from which he was to be shipped home an invalid, a plaintive, "Did I displease you, Mr. Higginson? Won't you tell me how?"

He had never met Emily, but recounted to Helen the description she'd sent him of herself, eyes "like sherry in the glass that the guest leaves" and hair, "bold like the chestnut burr."

"But what did you think of her work?" Helen wanted to know. He'd found it "strange, rather idealistic."

"'Too bad for blessing and too good for banning?'" she persisted, remembering a phrase from his advice article. He shook his head. Emily had never published or wanted to publish her verses; her only wish was to know if they "breathed."

Helen wanted nothing more than to publish — as often as possible. She saw in Higginson's style a model for her own. Using his *Outdoor Papers* as a guide, she set out to take them apart word by word, sentence by sentence, experimenting to see if she could take out a word or transpose a clause without destroying their perfection. "I shall never write a sentence, so long as I live, without studying it over from the standpoint of whether you think it could be bettered," she assured him.

He was surprised by the rapidity with which Helen wrote, covering large sheets of paper with a pencil — pen and ink were too slow for her. Yet for all her quickness, she was a patient and ruthless editor of her own work and a good critic of others.

Looking back later at that happy time, Higginson wrote: "She entered with the enthusiasm of a child upon her new work. She distrusted herself, was at first fearful of each new undertaking, yet was eager to try everything, and the moment each new plunge was taken lost all fear. I remember the surprise with which she received the suggestion that no doubt publishers would be happy to send her their books if she would only review them; and her delight as in a new world, when she opened the first parcels." A goal that long eluded her was publication in *Atlantic Monthly*. There were rejections, and Helen feared her work would never be good enough for the prestigious journal. Then one day Higginson read her latest poem, "Coronation," and insisted upon submitting it for her.

Helen was delighted, but her innate business instincts surfaced when she named her fee. "It was a high price for a newcomer to demand," he said later, "but she was inexorable, including rather curiously among her traits that of being an excellent business woman, and getting for her wares the price she set upon them. Fields reread it once, and exclaimed, 'It's a good poem'; then read it again, and said, 'it's a *devilish* good poem,' and accepted it without hesitation."

Before long the hard bargains Helen drove were a legend among editors. "Cash is a vile article," she admitted to the *Atlantic* editor James Thomas Fields. Then she added, "But there is one thing viler; and that is a purse without any cash in it." More than once she stated her sentiments succinctly: "I don't write for money, I write for love — I *print* for money." She was also quick to plant her sentiments in the mouths of her fictional heroines. ("If selling is an honorable business for men, it ought to be for women and girls," one protagonist argued.)

Adamant as she was about equal pay for women, Helen was critical of what she considered professional feminists. Higginson remembered, "Professedly abhorring woman's suffrage, she went with me to a convention on that subject in New York, under express contract to write a satirical report in a leading newspaper but was so instantly won over — as many another has been — by the sweet voice of Lucy Stone, that she defaulted as a correspondent, saying to me, 'Do you suppose I ever could write against anything to which that woman wishes done?'"

No judgments were sacred to Helen, least of all her own. Warm, generous, impulsive, she was open-minded and not at all reticent about admitting her own lapses. She didn't approve of women lecturers — until she encountered Anna Leonowens. It was exciting to meet the woman whose book she'd earlier reviewed and to hear first hand of the exciting experiences in Siam that had inspired it. Anna was lovely and charming. She had something to say, and Helen thought she should say it — to large audiences. Within a month, Helen had arranged a lecture date for her new friend at the Newport Opera House, written advance newspaper publicity, and was not only selling tickets herself, but prevailing on her astonished friends to sell them. Even the liberal Higginson was shocked by it. The love story of Boon, the runaway harem girl, struck him as being in very bad taste. Helen firmly disagreed and eventually made the story into a long poem. Neither would have believed that the tale of the Siamese sojourn would one day be rewritten as the bestseller *Anna and the King of Siam* and later made into the musical *The King and I*.

Higginson found Helen's blend of prejudice and generosity curiously charming. Knowing that she had briefly owned a slave during her early married days, he insisted that she accompany him to a "jubilee meeting of the colored people of Newport after emancipation." Helen came away, he said, "full of enthusiasm and sympathy, with much contrition as to things she had previously said and done." She did, however, balk at the idea that a well-educated young quadroon might move into the Dame boardinghouse. When Higginson invited the woman to tea, Helen, at first reluctant to attend, was so charmed by her that the two became close friends as well as housemates.

The pattern of Helen's relationship with Higginson was established early. That it was a passionate friendship kept from complete fulfillment only by his sense of obligation to Mary seems obvious. In May of 1866, only three months after Helen's move to Newport, *Nation* published another of her poems. Though the title was "The Burial Service," the subject was not death but renunciation. It began:

> To this burying
> We come alone — you and I — not with our dead,
> But with our dearest living; O, could mortal tread
> Be unfaltering!

There was no signature, not even H. H., after the conclusion:

> *To Christ's protection*
> *Now let us leave it — the tomb and the key! He*
> *Will remember us if there may ever be*
> *Resurrection!*

Not long afterward Helen made a sentimental visit to Brattleboro, Vermont, the village where Higginson's siblings lived. In the fall she was back in Newport acting as his hostess at a musicale while Mary remained upstairs in her chair. It was Helen who planned the decorations — great masses of fall flowers and bright foliage. A love of nature was only one of the many things she and Higginson shared.

As before, the two were much together, but by the following summer Helen was off again. It was a pattern that continued for five years, broken only in November 1868 when she left rather suddenly for Europe and remained away until February 1870. When Helen had been gone a full year, Higginson wrote in his journal: "Two things I miss that gave me happiness a year ago. One is *Malbone* [his current novel] is bad — the other a dream."

During this period Helen published the first of a number of popular novels written under the pseudonym Saxe Holm and never publicly acknowledged. Most share a recurrent theme — unhappy marriages with true love stifled by obligation. The heroine, often a writer, sometimes removes herself from temptation by going to Europe.

If Helen couldn't have the life she desired, she was at least learning to make the best of things. Winters were bittersweet, possibly romantic, summers pleasant mountain rambles in and around New England. Invariably she returned in the fall, preceded by great trunks of pressed ferns and flowers and autumn leaves that she distributed among friends during the bleak winters.

Those roving sojourns may have revealed other aspects of Helen's character as well — to be discreetly hinted at by Higginson after her death. "So ardent were her sympathies," he would one day eulogize, "that everything took color and form from her personal ties; and her readiness to form these ties with persons of all ages, both sexes and every condition not only afforded some of her greatest joys, but also brought the greatest perils to her life; often involving misconception, perplexity, and keen disappointment to herself and others. Her friendships with men had the frankness and openness that most women show only to one another; and her friendships with women had the romance and ideal atmosphere which her sex usually reserves for men. There was an utterly exotic and even tropical side of her nature, strangely mingled with the traits that came from her New England blood."

Higginson had firsthand knowledge of some painful consequences that Helen suffered. "Where her sympathy went, even in the least degree, there she was ready to give all she had — attention, time, trouble, money, popularity, reputation — and this with only too little thought of the morrow," he recalled. "The result was found not merely in many unreasonable requests, but in inconvenient and unlooked for expectations. During the middle period of her life there was never any security that the morning postman might not bring an impassioned letter from some enamored young girl, proposing to come and spend her life with her benefactress; or a proffer of hand and heart from some worthy man, with whom she had mistakenly supposed herself to be on a footing of the plainest good fellowship. It sometimes taxed all great resources of kindness and ready wit to extract herself from such entanglements; and she never could be made to understand how they had come about or why others succeeded them."

He seems to have understood her very well — an incredibly resilient woman, something of a flirt who frequently got more than she bargained for. He would write with rueful tenderness more than twenty years later, "She had great virtues, marked inconsistencies, and plenty of fascinating faults that came near to virtues." If he could be nothing more, Higginson was secure in his position as her closest confidant. Helen trusted him implicitly, pledging him to burn all her letters in the event of her death. It was a wise course, he wrote later, "not without reason, for she lived in the moment & was a most hazardous correspondent."

Under Thomas Higginson's tutelage, Helen had become a prolific writer, turning out a stream of poems, articles, and finally novels. She wrote with elegance and emotion, her independence giving zest to her opinions. Helen's heroines were much like she was, strong individualists often in conflict with the conventions of the time.

Helen's own life had taken on many of the qualities of a novel. If she didn't care for a plot or a character, if a situation became too confining, she could always change it. And that was exactly what she planned to do.

CHAPTER FOUR

California Collage

Broad, still, and soft — the prairie reminded Helen of the sea as it swirled by. Reaching for the familiar pad of yellow writing paper on the seat beside her, she picked up her pencil and began to write: "'Three nights and four days in the cars!' these words hurt us and hindered our rest. What should we eat and drink and wherewithal should we put our clothes? No scripture was strong enough to calm our anxious thoughts, no friend's experience of comfort enough to disarm our fears. 'Dust is dust,' said we, 'and railroad is railroad.' All resort cooking in America is intolerable. We shall be wretched; however we will go."

The lady protested far too much. She loved travel and lived in a state of constant anticipation with trunks and valises at the ready. Train, boat, or stagecoach — nothing was too arduous for her to undertake with vitality and enthusiasm.

The current journey was in fact a dream come true. Helen and her closest woman friend, Sarah Woolsey, were on their way to California. It was expensive — round-trip tickets on the Union and Central Pacific just under three hundred dollars. Everything else — drawing rooms, berths, meals, hotels, carriages, guides, horses — was extra. Helen had estimated that the two-month trip would cost each of them between seven and eight hundred dollars. Fortunately her success was such that money was not a prime consideration.

She had developed a sense of what people wanted to read and possessed the talent and drive to create it. Following the success of her first Saxe Holm novel came *Bits of Travel,* a collection of European sketches. One reviewer hailed the travelogue as "the work of genius." Though *Nation* thought it "spoiled by too much vivacity," Scribner's insisted that "no woman in America showed as much promise as H. H."

Sarah Woolsey, a gifted amateur, had been critiqued and encouraged by her friend. At Helen's insistence she wrote a children's book, which was submitted and sold, fetching her "a pretty penny." She, too, could afford to splurge and was ready to join Helen in an adventure.

Boarding the train in New York on May 8, 1872, they settled into their private drawing room surrounded by "life preservers" that had been pressed upon them by friends — baskets filled with fruit, chicken, orange marmalade, and Albert biscuits. It was a cozy, comfortable place with luxurious reclining chairs and plenty of room for their many bags and bundles. Later Helen recalled the happiness of the moment: "A perplexing sense of domesticity crept over us as we settled into corners, hung up our cologne bottles and missed the cat!" Such complacency couldn't last.

After Ogden there was no more drawing-room service, and they were forced to content themselves with a Pullman car filled to capacity with other travelers. Never one to mask her feelings, Helen shared them with her reading public: "I dislike the sleeping-car section more than I ever have disliked, ever shall dislike, or ever can dislike anything in the world."

Then she explained why: "Fancy a mattress laid on the bottom shelf in your cupboard and the cupboard door shut. You have previously made a choice among your possessions of which ones you must have, and will therefore keep all night on the foot of your bed (that is, on your own feet). Accurate memory and judicious selection under such circumstances are impossible. No sooner is the cupboard door shut than you remember that several indispensable articles are under the shelf. But the door is locked, and you can't get out. By which I mean that the porter has put up the curtain in front of your section, and of the opposite section, and you have partially undressed, and you can't step out into the narrow aisle without encountering the English gentleman who is going by to heat water on the stove at the end of the car; and, even if you didn't encounter him, you can't get your things which have been stowed away under your shelf unless you lie down at full length on the floor because most of the floor is under your opposite neighbor's shelf. So I said the door was locked simply to express the hopelessness of the situation. Then you sit cross-legged on your bed; because, of course, you can't sit on the edge of the shelf after the cupboard door is shut — that is, the curtain is put up so close to the edge of your bed that, if you sit there in the natural human manner, your knees and feet will be in the way of the English gentleman when he passes. . . ."

It was a lot to ask of a Victorian lady with her buttons and bows, her stays, corsets, and laces, nor was it all she had to endure. "Be as silent, as unsocial, as surly as you please, you cannot avoid being more or less impressed by the magnetism of every human being in the car," she advised her readers. "Their faces attract or repell; you like, you dislike, you wonder, you pity, you resent, you loathe. In the course of twenty-four hours you have expended a great deal of nerve force to no purpose. . . ."

Helen's ordeal in the "cars" was an experience that would, of course, find its way into a book, *Bits of Travel at Home*. Despite her frankness, it had the effect of stimulating western train travel. Luxurious it wasn't, but the author found compensation in the rich prairie lands that unrolled themselves, smiled, and fled.

Not long after crossing the Platte River, Helen caught sight of a real Indian. The experience was an unlikely preface to her ultimate dedication. "We were told it was a woman," she wrote, "it was apparently made of old India-rubber, much soaked, seamed and torn. It was

thatched at the top with a heavy roof of black hair which
hung down from a ridge-like line in the middle. It moved
about on brown, bony, stalking members for which no
experience furnishes a name."

Helen shrank from the woman's long, grasping fingers
as she might "from the claws of a bear." She shut her
eyes and turned away from the "most abject, loathly
living thing" she'd ever seen. But then she looked again
and saw the baby — "gleaming out from under a ragged
arch of basket-work, a smooth, shining soft face, brown
as a nut, sweet, happy, innocent and confident."
Swathed in a solid roll and strapped to a flat board
fastened to its mother's back, the infant was helpless as
a mummy — body, legs, arms, and feet bandaged tightly;
but Helen saw that "its great, soft, black eyes looked
fearlessly at everybody" and thought "it as genuine and
blessed a baby as any woman ever bore."

Others had noticed the child as well. Idle thoughtless
passengers jeered at the squaw, saying: "Sell us the
papoose." "Give you greenbacks for the papoose."
Then, and not until then, Helen saw what she recognized
as a human look in the "India-rubber face." The
woman's eyes could flash, the mouth show scorn.

As always with Helen, it was the intimate, personal
aspect of need or injustice that caught her attention and
aroused her feelings. Elegant and fastidious, she had no
use for dirt and little understanding or sympathy for dirty
people, whatever their circumstances. It had been the
baby that had awakened her concern and opened her
purse.

At last the plains, deserts, and mountains were
crossed. The train was descending into Colfax, California,
then a bustling, thriving city nestling in the foothills of
the Sierra. It had been "months" since breakfast, and
Helen and Sarah were cheered by the sight of men and
boys running from car to car with baskets of ripe
strawberries to sell along with magnificent red roses.

In the station colorful placards advertised circuses and concerts; yellow stagecoaches stood ready to take people to such places as "You Bet" and "Red Dog." Summer and history were beckoning.

They found Sacramento noisy — "hacks, hotels, daily papers and all," then soon their train was threading its way between great masses of waving blooms. It seemed to Helen, awestruck by the impact of so much yellow lupine and mustard, that "California's hidden gold had grown impatient of darkness and burst into flower." The valley widened to plains, and the snow-topped mountains behind them grew lower and dimmer and bluer until they fell below the horizon line.

And then at last the bustle and confusion of the Oakland ferry terminal. It seemed strange to have crossed the width of America — forests, prairies, deserts, mountains — only to be ferried to the continent's edge. As always, it was people and personalities that made the experience real to Helen. In the jostling crowd were two brothers searching for one another. They'd not met in twenty years. How could the boys-become-men recognize each other? They couldn't. Finally it was an accidental word, overheard, that revealed them to each other.

She studied their faces, "singularly upright, sweet faces both of them; faces that one could trust on sight and love on knowledge." The brother that had journeyed from the East was her friend from the train; the brother who stood waiting on the western shore was his twin, but looked twenty years older. "There are spaces wider than lands can measure or the seas fill," she wrote later. "This was the moment, after all, and this was the thing which will always live in my memory as significant of crossing the continent."

Helen didn't think much of San Francisco. "There is nothing to the City to detain the traveler many days," she advised. (She hadn't cared much for Paris either — "New York grown up, graduated and with a diploma.") It was the natural beauty of California that thrilled her, each place seemingly more spectacular than the one before. Nothing had prepared her for the sunset on the Golden Gate Bay as she sailed toward Vallejo with Tamalpais a yellow mist on her left and Diablo a purple cloud on her right.

As they reached the edge of the Napa Valley and saw yellow grain and green vines stretching for miles on either side, the vista broken at last only by mountains, she exclaimed: "Surely there can be no such other valley as this in California!" But no, she was told, Napa was a small affair, pretty enough, but nothing beside the San Joaquin, the great central valley fifty miles wide and three hundred miles long.

Her visit to Santa Cruz was another in a series of delightful surprises: "First an hour in the cars, running southward through the Santa Clara Valley — parks and rich men's houses, wheat and oats, and windmills by the dozens; then, just at sunset, San Jose, another of the sacred old mission towns. It lies low, between two mountain ranges. It is shady and straight and full of flowers. There are public gardens with round tables under the trees, with little ponds, and boats, and targets and jumping boards." But that was nothing compared to Santa Cruz itself, "the sweetest of the seaside places." And then there was the grandeur of Lake Tahoe and the magnificence of Big Trees of Calaveras.

Finally, her favorite was Yosemite, which she insisted upon calling by its original Indian name, Ah-Wah-Ne. She was scornful of the settlers who, not content with chasing off the Indian inhabitants of the valley, had attempted to eradicate their very spirit.

Natives had tried to discourage Helen and Sarah from going to Yosemite, insisting that it was far too primitive for them. Fortunately the women persevered. The place, they found, had all the adventure and sense of pioneering that they'd dreamed about. Accommodations were primitive, riding trails precipitous, but neither thought of complaining. They would never forget the splendor of the mountains or the mighty roar of Ah-Wah-Ne Falls.

Helen vowed to come again. She would return the very next summer to study the old missions, she promised, little dreaming that it would be ten years before she returned, and then for a far greater purpose than she could ever have imagined.

CHAPTER FIVE

A Fallen Angel

Helen returned home to find her world in an uproar. It was 1872 and no American woman could vote, yet the free-spirited journalist Victoria · Woodhull had announced her candidacy for the presidency. Her platform was equal rights for women.

Helen had little sympathy for Woodhull and the other highly visible feminists of the day. She herself felt more than equal. As a woman rapidly rising to the top of her profession, one who traveled at will both alone and with the friends of her choice, an individualist who enjoyed the respect and camaraderie of both sexes, she lacked only what Woodhull and other women's rights advocates appeared to disdain. Helen craved a family.

"Wanted — a Home," her protest against what she considered "the wrong side of the Women's Rights Movement," soon appeared in the *Hartford Courant*. With bewilderment as well as indignation, she wrote, "There is an evil fashion of speech which says it is a narrowing and narrow life that a woman leads who cares only for her husband and children; that a higher, more imperative thing is that she herself be developed to the utmost. . . ." The premise confounded Helen, who thought so often of the husband and children who had been taken from her.

Perhaps she thought as well of Higginson and the children she might have had with him. She was back at the Dame boardinghouse once again, thrown into daily contact with Higginson. It was a dreary winter. Helen was often ill, plagued with bronchial problems that developed into diphtheria.

In the spring she rallied sufficiently to plan a return trip to California, and she began a vigorous correspondence with several publishers importuning them to provide free passes for her. It was only right, she reasoned. Hadn't her glowing accounts of California stimulated tourist interest in that far-off place, and wasn't she promising still more articles? Helen had in mind to take May Alcott (sister of Louisa May and prototype of Amy in *Little Women*) with her, but when weeks elapsed and no passes were forthcoming, May — who had no money of her own — happily accepted a thousand dollars scraped together by Louisa and went off to study art in London.

Depressed and disappointed, Helen lacked the strength for a long trip alone, but still longed for a change of scene. At last she wrote to her old friend Emily Dickinson. Was there a "dry and clean" boardinghouse in Amherst where she could stay? Emily, as always, responded immediately, informing her of a place with "no dampness." She assured Helen that it must be fine because cousins of hers who were "very timid themselves" stayed there.

Despite the opinion of Emily's timid cousins, the result was a "most disastrous week" for Helen. Ill before she started, the trip exhausted her to the point that she "was prostrated in twelve hours." The place was not only damp, but also stifling. She would not have survived, Helen later insisted, without the aid of Dr. Hamilton J. Cate, who "saved" her life.

Like Higginson, the Hawthornes, and Harriet Beecher Stowe, Helen had caught the enthusiasm for homeopathic medicine prevalent at the time. Cate's method was to prescribe pills containing toxins to counteract the germs that he believed were overwhelming her system. Perhaps he saved her life, perhaps not; he most certainly changed its course by emphatically urging her to try the Colorado climate.

Friends were shocked. Colorado was considered a wild, barbarous place with its Indian massacres and train robberies. Helen debated, well aware that she was forty-two — older now by four years than her mother had been when she had died. She feared that her persistent ailments presaged the beginning of a similar illness. The salubrious effect of the Colorado climate on respiratory ailments was currently being touted . . . once again her spirits rose at the prospect of some place new.

Never one to worry about convention, Helen set off November 17 accompanied by her maid and Dr. Cate. Without his consistent optimism she would probably have taken the first train back. Colorado was awful, the plains "blank, bald, a pitiless gray, under a gray November sky." Denver was "horrible," and, to make matters worse, she had a new cold. Undaunted, the indefatigable Cate urged her to try the new town of Colorado Springs some seventy miles to the south.

Helen hated settling into "Deadman's Row" — a line of connected portable houses that had been shipped in from Chicago to accommodate the invalid population attracted by the climate. She felt a measure of relief when a vacancy occurred at the newly constructed Colorado Springs Hotel, but the move did little to improve her mood. "One might die of such a place alone," she commented dyspeptically, "but death by disease would be more natural." Having crossed much of the country to find "a climate which would not kill," she felt even sicker and more despondent than before. Colorado Springs was "small, straight, new, treeless." It lay between "a dark range of mountains, snow-topped, rocky-walled, stern, cruel, relentless and a bleak, unrelieved desolate plain." Worst of all was the dust. It sifted in through windows and doors, settling everywhere until it seemed to penetrate her very soul.

Then, just when Helen felt she could stand it no longer, the first snow fell and the "delicious winter weather" cleared the air. She could open her windows at night and look out at a towering mountain range that included Pike's Peak, nearly fifteen thousand feet high. Almost immediately her cold vanished, her throat improved, and Dr. Cate, having fulfilled his destiny in Helen's life, returned to Amherst.

The doctor had restricted Helen's diet to "gruel and iron pills," and even though she had no need to go to the dining room for those, she was far too convivial to remain in her rooms at meal-times. Despite the fact that it was described as "the most elegant hostelry between Chicago and San Francisco," the Colorado Springs Hotel was little more than a large boardinghouse. Seated among six "agreeable talkers," she was happily reminded of her Newport companions — with one significant difference. Here the most attractive male guest was unmarried. The seventh tablemate, William Sharpless Jackson, wasn't an agreeable talker at all. He was of the strong silent variety, benignly oblivious to all the chatter going on around him. During conversational lulls, Helen studied Jackson — a big man with deep-set eyes and a touch of gray in his heavy beard and whiskers. She was curious about him, wondering what his story might be.

Possibly William sensed Helen's disappointment in Colorado — a place he'd come to love — and couldn't resist an opportunity to proselytize; or perhaps this quiet man was drawn to the worldly stranger, with her dramatic sense of style and warm, vivacious manner. Very soon after their initial meeting, he invited her to ride with him into the countryside.

It was an experience that Helen would remember always. Some of it she recorded later in the article, "A Winter Morning at Colorado Springs." Though it was December 14, 1873, she found it a season "that woos and warms" like June. Wrapped in furs, she leaned back in William's open carriage and admired his magnificent white horses prancing "like frolicsome kittens." They rode through the Ute Pass, admiring the beauty of the creek that flowed alongside. There was an otherworldly quality about it all. "Ice bridges, ice arches," she later wrote, "ice veils over little falls," and in the center, reaching almost to the rushing stream, hung "one pendant globule, pear-shaped, flashing like a diamond."

William reined in and they dismounted. Taking his hand, Helen stepped to the edge of a sharp rock where they could sit in the warm, noonday sun. Looking down "into the huge crystal bowl — solid white snow at the bottom and frost-work up the sides," she listened as Jackson told her the story of his life. He was a little more than five years younger than she, born to a Pennsylvania Quaker family on January 16, 1836. Apprenticed as a boy to an agricultural machinist, there'd been no opportunity to acquire a formal education; but Jackson had a quick mind and knew what he wanted. Once his period of indenture had been completed, he'd gone to work for a railway car building company, finally working his way up to treasurer of the Superior and Mississippi Railroad. Then three years ago he'd shocked everyone by giving it all up to come west.

Helen nodded sympathetically. She understood his wanderlust well and wasn't surprised to learn that the move had worked out well for him. The modest, mild-mannered man beside her was not only vice president of the Denver and Rio Grande Railroad, but founder and president of a bank in Colorado Springs as well. Later she wrote that they had galloped home "seven miles to the hour." The sun was bright, the snow dazzling. It was a day she would never forget.

There were many outings. By April Helen had sent east for her trunks. In one article on Colorado Springs, she enthused, "That plain and those mountains are to me wellnigh the fairest spot on earth." But when her friend William Hayes Ward, editor of the *New York Independent,* inquired about a rumored romance, she was evasive. Without ever mentioning Jackson by name, Helen admitted that the man in question "was very well known in the area." She didn't mind confiding that she "felt leery of taking such a major step."

Actually the item linking them had first appeared in the *Rocky Mountain News,* taking her totally by surprise. With Helen's studious avoidance of any sort of notoriety, small-town gossip was bad enough. The knowledge that the story had been picked up by eastern papers appalled her. It was an "impudent paragraph," she fumed to Will.

A simple, uncomplicated man, Jackson had no idea what all the fuss was about. He wanted to marry Helen and didn't care who knew it. She was flattered but hesitant. Will was very possibly the best catch in the territory. There was no question that he could offer her peace and security, but there was the difference in their ages and backgrounds to consider and the possibility that he might one day regret not having children. Besides, Helen had been a widow for ten years and was used to coming and going as she pleased. "I have commitments to my publishers," she evaded.

"I'll wait," he replied.

Helen went east that summer to visit friends, among them Higginson. Mary, though as much an invalid as ever, clung tenaciously to life. Helen imagined that she would probably outlive them all and returned to Colorado Springs. Still, it was more than a year before she agreed to marry Will.

Once again she had selected the autumn for her nuptials: October 22, 1875, at her sister Ann's home in Wolfeboro, New Hampshire. This time the bride wore green and was married outdoors under a canopy of scarlet-leaved maples.

Emily Dickinson, who corresponded with both Helen and Higginson and who possibly sensed more than either realized, responded to her friend's marriage in a curious manner. Following a brief line of congratulations, she cryptically added a stanza:

> *Who flees from the Spring*
> *The Spring avenging fling*
> *To Dooms of Balm*

Startled, Helen responded immediately, "I do wish I knew what 'Dooms' you meant. . . . " If Emily explained herself, the letter didn't survive.

She informed William Hayes Ward of her marriage by sending him a new calling card imprinted with the names Mr. and Mrs. William S. Jackson. The editor of the *Independent,* and incurable punster, responded: "If a man can not find a wife on earth he should go to Helen Hunt."

Her immediate reply:

Dear Mr. Ward:
    Fallen angels are very lovable. I advise every man to go to the same place in search.

Yours truly,
Mrs. Jackson

CHAPTER SIX

Helen of Colorado

Will believed he'd bought a showplace for his bride.
Helen could have cried. She thought the gingerbread
Gothic was hopeless. All her life she'd managed to
transform her surroundings, again and again taking just
two rented rooms and turning them into a haven that
reflected her own colorful personality and love of beauty.
Now her friends were speculating about what she'd do
with a real home — a place of her very own.

The first thing Helen did was turn it all around. The
house had been constructed so that the only view of
Cheyenne Mountain — surely one of the most spectacular
views she had seen — was from the kitchen window. And
she knew she wouldn't be spending much time *there*.

By the time she had finished, the entrance no longer
faced Weber Street. Their address was now 228 East
Kiowa, and the former backporch and kitchen had been
transformed into a large living room with a commanding
view of a mountain range that included not only
Cheyenne Mountain but Pike's Peak as well. The house
now was really a showplace, with "flirtation corners,"
massive fireplaces, cozy alcoves, galleries to display
Helen's treasures, and floor-to-ceiling shelves for books.
Special innovations she designed included revolving
tables that displayed magazines and held still more
books. Visitors from the East found vines and leaves
framing pictures and windows, piñon logs blazing in the
stone fireplaces. Tables were festooned with fresh flow-

ers, and individual bouquets marked each place. One guest remembered a luncheon with twenty-three different varieties of wildflowers decorating the house.

Unfortunately those treasured eastern companions were not able to make the long trip often, and Helen — try as she might — could not find their like in Colorado Springs. The stimulation she craved was lacking. In addition, the nouveau society of the town thought her something of a snob — all those effete eastern magazines lying about and so *many* books. She was a bit odd too, insisting upon sleeping with her head to the north just like an Indian. And then there was the matter of Helen's refusal to attend church. Tentative attempts to bring her into the fold went unrewarded.

Helen began a chapter in *Bits of Travel at Home* by stating, "There are in Colorado Springs seven places of worship, the Episcopal, Methodist, Baptist, Presbyterian, Congregational, and Unitarian churches, and Cheyenne Canyon." Irate townspeople thought she might just as well have listed fifty places of worship, enumerating all the mountaintops and valleys in the area that she was in the habit of visiting on the Sabbath day.

The Presbyterian church was just across the street from Helen's house. Worshipers complained of the sight and sound of her "most every Sabbath going on an excursion or picnic." A prominent member of the Episcopal church complained that not only did she herself picnic on Sundays, but she also invited his daughters to go with her.

Helen and God had come to terms years before. Now she found the Great Spirit in the secluded recesses of Cheyenne Canyon, where she frequently rode on her sure-footed burrow. Gradually over the years she'd mastered her own life, and now she made her own rules. The instant intimacy of small-town life was not for her. Fresh, witty, and warm, she was popular when she chose to be, but she didn't always make that choice.

But if the self-styled socialites of Colorado Springs were sometimes boring, the "characters" of the area were not. Some invariably found their way into Helen's sketches. "Grandma" Varner was one, and years later that pioneer woman would have her own tale to tell to a writer from *The Overland Monthly*. By then Mrs. Varner was eighty-nine and blind, but she still wore a scarf about her neck — crossed at the waist Quaker style — and combed her hair with the faultless precision of lifetime.

"I remember Mrs. Jackson just as plain as I do my mother," she said of her first encounter more than three decades earlier. "It was years ago when they undertook to build the new railroad out from Colorado Springs. I had only a little while before taken [*sic*] Tommy out with me to Colorado, for he was kind of delicate like, and I lived in fear of losing him. He was a slip of a boy about sixteen, and he was all the help he could be to me, but times were hard. We took our wagon and tried to follow the men along the road. Tommy earning money hauling for them and I doing their washing and mending. The day I met Mrs. Jackson stands out in my memory as bringing into my life a character altogether new. She was the first person who was ever really kind to me.

"One day while I had the clothes a boiling over the fire beside the wagon-box where we lived, I noticed that I was out of wood, and I had to go and gather some so that my clothes might be dried that night. I was walking down the road with my arms filled with twigs and wood when I saw the strange woman. She seemed kind of interested in me but I was just a little bit annoyed for I had my work to do and did not want to be disturbed.

"A woman I knew pretty well introduced her as Mrs. Jackson and I stood and talked a minute and then told her if she wanted to visit with me she'd have to sit down and let me go ahead with my work. I was out of money and had to get the washing done as quick as I could to get a dollar or two. While I worked she talked to me and asked me many questions. I did not think I was very agreeable to her, but as she left she gave me $2 and asked me to come and see her when I went to Colorado Springs.

"I never had any intention of going to see her, for I knew she was a grand lady, but when the work gave out in the mountains, Tommy and I went to the Springs. There I took in washing for some people in Consumption Row and Tommy he ran chores for others. One day Mrs. Jackson was down in that part of town doing some charity work when she heard of Tommy.

"She wondered right away if it was my boy and looked us up. She called and I was mortified to death because there was no fire. I told the visitor that Tommy must have forgotten to order coal and she said she didn't mind the cold, but a little later that day a ton of coal was delivered to us, a present from her. She wanted us to come over to her house that night, and she had her cook give us a basket full of good things to take home." Mrs. Varner "took to going over often" after that, never dreaming that her stories would find their way into print.

At the time her thoughts centered entirely around Tommy. "He's learning," she'd told Helen, "he's learning to do for hisself. He's a real good boy and he's getting stronger every day. He's getting his health real firm, 'n that's all I want. Tain't any matter what becomes of me, if I can only get Tommy started all right." And, partially with Helen's help, she had accomplished that. It would be sixteen years before Mrs. Varner learned that her story had been incorporated into the book *Bits of Travel at Home*. She was thrilled by this fragment of immortality and read and reread the account as long as her eyesight permitted.

Perhaps the differences between Will and Helen first became apparent when he decided to run for senator from Colorado. Sickened by a decade of political corruption — impeachments and near impeachments, shocking scandals, blatant miscarriages of private justice and public funds — Helen was horrified. And when her editor friend William Hayes Ward wrote wishing Will success in his venture, she replied with her usual candor: "Every election year is a bad one, human nature being what it is. I believe that our institutions will always bring to the surface of political power the scum of the land. Now I know these are unpopular views so I rarely air them but you have forced me to declare myself. To see my husband in that crew of liars and psychopaths will almost kill me." Her consolation, she said, was that "votes are bought and sold in Colorado and he will not buy a vote. So I think he will be defeated."

Though Will's motives were impeccable and his objectives honest, he was a practical man and lived in the available world. He neither sought nor expected miracles of reform, but Helen's stance was a keen disappointment. Will had expected his stylish, socially adept bride to be at his side during the campaign. She demurred whenever possible. Not only was his cause anathema to her, but her nerves shrank from the "tangled vibrations" of crowds. She was frustrated by the pull between his needs and desires and her own. To Helen, political socializing was senseless, if not dishonest; and, even worse, it cut into her writing time.

Hour after hour she sat at her desk scribbling, occasionally looking up from her yellow notepad to admire the bold outline of Cheyenne Mountain. Often it seemed the massive bastion of Pike's Peak was a kind of beacon. The novel that evolved that difficult winter was *Mercy Philbrick's Choice,* the story of a woman very like herself — pragmatic, energetic, resilient, an individualist who "did things, said things and felt things with the instantaneous intensity of the poetic temperament," and sometimes regretted them. Helen was most certainly speaking for herself when her heroine philosophized, "The loneliness of intense individuality is the loneliest loneliness in the world — a loneliness which crowds only aggravate."

There were other similarities. Mercy was a widow who loved and was loved by a man emotionally chained to an invalid—in this instance, his mother. An older man, Parson Dorrance, also loved Mercy. Like Higginson, he was a former clergyman-turned-man-of-letters who inspired her to become a professional writer. There was tragedy latent in this relationship as well. Dorrance had been married to a once "marvelous" woman who "sank into a hopeless invalidism,—an invalidism all the more difficult to bear, and to be borne with, that it took the shape of distressing nervous maladies which no medical skill could alleviate. The brilliant mind became almost a wreck, and yet retained a preternatural restlessness and activity. Many regarded her condition as insanity, and believed that Mr. Dorrance erred in not giving her up to the care of those making mental disorders a specialty. But his love and patience were untiring. . . ." In the novel Parson Dorrance, unlike poor Higginson, was at last a widower and free to marry Mercy. It was she, chained by love to the other prisoner, who couldn't marry him.

One wonders what Thomas and Mary Higginson would have thought had they guessed the authorship. Small wonder the novel went unsigned. Helen was delighted when Roberts Brothers of Boston approached her to launch their "No Name" Series. The plan was to bring out a number of anonymous books written, as the circular advertised, by authors "of great unknown." The idea of provoking readers into a kind of guessing game proved to be the most financially rewarding publishing scheme of the decade, and once again Helen had a success on her hands.

Helen couldn't and didn't write all the time. In her journal there were often notations: "Went riding with Will, a perfect day." And in one of her nature sketches, she referred to him obliquely: "There is a part of Cheyenne Mountain which I and one other have come to call 'our garden.' When we drive down from 'our garden,' there is seldom room for another flower in our carriage. The top thrown back is filled, the space in front of the driver is filled, and our laps are filled with the more delicate blossoms. We look as if we were on our way to the ceremonies of Decoration Day. So we are but it is the joy of life we decorate — not the sacred sadness of death."

These days were especially precious to Helen, for the differences between her and Will that she had sensed before their marriage were becoming more and more apparent. Both meant well, each taking pride in the achievements of the other; but more and more frequently the demands of their careers took them in different directions. Helen was vastly relieved when Will lost the election; but if she had thought the void in his life would bring them closer, she was mistaken. Jackson had been a bachelor for thirty-nine years; like herself, he was independent, accustomed to coming and going as he pleased. Often he was away on railroad or banking business, but even when he was at home, it was sometimes as if a chasm divided them.

Though Will had recently been asked to serve on the Board of Trustees of Colorado College and was a member of the town's school board, his interest was entirely administrative. There was little of the intellectual in him, no appreciation for poetry or a clever turn of phrase. Clearly no helpful criticism could be expected from Will, and — canny as he was with his own affairs — he had no understanding of publishing strategies. Helen must often have thought of Higginson and longed for his advice and companionship.

Then, two years after Helen's marriage, Mary Higginson died suddenly. Within a year Higginson had announced his engagement to Mary Potter Thacher, a woman of thirty-four to his fifty-five. The new Mary, Helen learned, had come into Higginson's life via her book of light essays. Her writing aspirations rested there. Not long after the announcement, the bride-elect admitted to Henry Wadsworth Longfellow, her uncle by marriage: "Even if I should not in future do much literary work on my account, I look forward with delight to helping him. Don't you think that will be much better fun?"

Later, while thanking him for his engagement gift, she confided: "'All things come round to him who will wait.' And now it seems to me that, with the greatest blessing a woman can have, all others are heaped upon me. I have always wanted a watch."

Naive, yes, but also healthy and nubile. Mary managed to produce, within a discreet period, the child Higginson had always longed for.

Helen had talent, Emily Dickinson genius. If Helen sensed the truth, she was nonetheless generous in her efforts to launch her friend. She was the first to recognize Emily's gifts and as far back as the early Newport days had urged Higginson to offer his assistance. He was, however, doubtful, hesitant; Emily's work was *strange*. It was only when Helen had been off in Europe for a year and he at loose ends that Higginson had reluctantly made a trip to Amherst to meet with her.

As it turned out, he spent most of the time quizzing Emily about Edward Hunt, Helen's late husband. Emily, possibly sensing where his real interests lay, twitted him a bit by referring to Hunt as the most interesting man she had ever seen. Higginson's reaction to this extreme enthusiasm about a man Emily had met only once is left to the imagination. His feelings toward her are a matter of record. "I never was with anyone who drained my nerve power so much," he complained. "Without touching her, she drew from me. I am glad not to live near her."

Helen was surprised by this description, but over the years would hear even worse reports. To many, Emily appeared pathetically withdrawn, eccentric, possibly even insane. She had become the "myth" of Amherst, a recluse who hadn't left the house since her thirty-fifth year. Refusing to be put off by gossip, Helen had written —shortly after her marriage and the receipt of Emily's cryptic "doom" poem— "I hope some day, somewhere I shall find you in a spot where we can know each other. . . ." She went on to urge: "You are a great poetess and it is wrong to the day you live in that you will not sing aloud. When you are what men call dead you will be sorry you were so stingy."

Emily's response was "intense surprise" that her friend would allow her work to be published. "How could you print a piece of your soul?" she asked. The two remained at an impasse. Both continued in their chosen lifestyles; Emily closeted in her room working and reworking tiny fragments of poems, Helen moving restlessly about the country — with and without her husband — prolifically pouring out poems, essays, sketches, short stories, and novels.

With time on her hands, Emily took their correspondence quite seriously. When her letters sometimes went unanswered, she invariably assumed that Helen was "offended." One of Helen's replies began: "How could you possibly have offended me? I am sorry that such an idea should have suggested itself to you. I have often thought of sending you a line, but there are only sixty minutes in an hour. There are not half enough."

Then Helen moved on to more important matters. She believed she'd at last found the means of luring her friend into print. Her own intense need for privacy enabled her to understand Emily's reticence. Once early in Helen's career, her delight at being accepted by *Atlantic* had been spoiled by that magazine's inadvertent printing of her name beneath her poem. For Helen, the anonymity of H. H. and the pseudonym Saxe Holm had been enough; Emily clearly required something more. Helen thought she'd found it in the "No Name" Series. Fourteen volumes had now been published in quick succession; and at her suggestion the publisher planned as a final offering an anthology of anonymous verse.

Enclosed in the letter was a circular advertising the upcoming *Masque of Poets*. Helen explained: "When the volume of verse is published in this series, I shall contribute to it; and I want to persuade you to. Surely, in the shelter of such *double* anonymousness as that will be, you need not shrink. I want to see some of your verses in print. Unless you forbid me, I will send some that I have. May I?. . . . . ."

Now it was Emily's turn to be silent. There was nothing for Helen to do but go to Amherst to persuade her. The atmosphere of dramatic eccentricity with which Emily surrounded herself had stimulated endless speculation. Mutual acquaintances warned: "It's a waste of time. Emily Dickinson never sees *anyone*." Even Lavinia Dickinson wasn't at all certain that her weird sister would admit Helen; the differences between them seemed vast. "Helen Hunt Jackson was a brilliant, dashing woman of the world, fearless and brave, while Emily was timid and refined, always shrinking from publicity," she would recall.

Helen did get in, and if she was appalled by the thin, wraithlike figure who admitted her, she didn't show it. In no time the two were eating Emily's homemade bread (her late father had called it her "only gift") and reminiscing about old times. Soon Helen had shifted the subject to poetry. She left believing that Emily had decided to contribute to *A Masque of Poets*.

Apparently there were second thoughts. Emily was soon appealing to Higginson: "Dear Friend—Are you willing to tell me what is right. Mrs. Jackson—of Colora-ado—was with me a few moments this week. . . . I said I was incapable and she seemed not to believe me . . . she was so sweetly noble I would regret to estrange her, and if you would be willing to give me a note saying you disapprove it, and thought me unfit, she would believe you——" His answer was noncommittal.

When days passed and no poems were forthcoming, Helen wrote from Ashfield, Massachusetts, where she was staying. She began by apologizing for having remarked that Emily lived too much away from the sunlight, "but truly you seemed so white and moth-like [and] your hand felt like such a wisp in mine that you fright-ened me—I like a great ox, talking to a white moth begging it to come and eat grass with me to see if it could turn itself into beef! How stupid. . . . You say you find great pleasure in reading my verses. Let somebody somewhere whom you do not know have the same pleasure in reading yours."

Eighteen months passed, and Helen, busy with the complex demands of her life, continued to be the same prodigal correspondent. At last Emily wrote asking if her face was "averted." She sent in lieu of a poem a photograph of her two-year-old nephew.

On April 29, 1878, Helen replied from Colorado Springs: "My face was not 'averted' in the least. It was only that I did not speak; and of my not speaking, I ought to be very much ashamed, and should be, if I had not got past being ashamed of my delinquencies in the matter of letter writing."

After a few random remarks, she returned to the central issue: "Would it be of any use to ask you once more for one or two of your poems, to come out in the volume of "no name" poetry which is to be published before long by Roberts Bros.? If you will give me permission I will copy them — sending them in my own handwriting — and promise never to tell anyone, not even the publishers, whose poems they are. Could you not bear this much publicity? Only you and I would recognize the poems. I wish very much that you would do this — and I think you would have much amusement in seeing to whom the critics, those shrewd guessers, would ascribe your verses."

She and Will would be traveling east later in the year, Helen said, and before closing asked to be remembered to an Amherst friend — then modified, "I was about to say 'When you see him,' but you never see anybody! Perhaps you have improved. . . ."

If Helen was not the most reliable of correspondents, she was very much a professional writer well aware of the meaning of a deadline. *A Masque of Poets* was scheduled for November publication. Copy was due immediately, and she was determined that at least one of Emily's poems be included. It's likely that in a wave of optimism she sent her favorite, sure for the moment that she could secure formal permission later.

In October she was back in Amherst. For a "lovely hour" (Emily's recollection) the two were closeted in the library while Will and Lavinia Dickinson struggled to find a common ground in the parlor. However "lovely" the hour, Helen was keenly aware that the book had already gone to press with Emily's poem included. The necessary permission had not been given.

On October 24 the Jacksons left Amherst, and the following day Helen wrote one last frantic note: "My dearest friend — Here comes the line I promised to send .... Now — will you send me the poem? No — will you let me send the "Success" which I know by heart — to Roberts Bros. for the *Masque of Poets?* If you will, it will give me great pleasure. I ask it as a personal favor to myself — Can you refuse the only thing I perhaps shall ever ask at your hands?"

Even an individual as insulated as Emily must have been was aware that a book with a publication date less than three weeks away had been completed long ago. Helen's message was more than a request, it was a desperate plea for help, understanding, and forgiveness.

And so in the end Helen got her way. Protest was now pointless; besides friendships were rare in Emily's life. Warm and scintillating — Helen was her window on the world, irreplaceable.

In late November *A Masque of Poets* appeared on the stands. It contained an unsigned verse by Emily Dickinson. It began:

> *Success is counted sweetest*
> *By those who ne'er succeed*

By Autumn 1879 Helen was at loose ends, unwilling or unable to conceal any longer her general dissatisfaction with the direction her life was taking. In May she'd written Emily, "The 'man I live with' (I suppose you recollect designating my husband by that curiously direct phrase) is in New York — and I am living alone."

Why Will hadn't taken her along on this business trip, one can only wonder. Helen consoled herself by remodeling the house once again — this time to include the indoor bathroom that he'd originally thought an unnecessary extravagance.

Perhaps some of Helen's thoughts were reflected in *Hetty's Strange History*, another of her "no name" novels. Like herself, Hetty was married to a man five years her junior. At first the union was a happy one; then Hetty began to brood about the difference in their ages. She studied her face and contrasted it with her husband's "fresh, manly beauty at forty years, in its perfect prime." At last it came to her "that, in living with her, he was being defrauded of happiness he nobly deserved." Hetty's solution was to pretend a fatal accident, assuming that, believing her drowned, her husband would be free to marry someone younger.

The book was provocative, controversial, the ethics of Hetty's actions debated in countless drawing rooms. Higginson, unaware of the author's identity, congratulated her in a review that ended, "The author is especially to be thanked for venturing boldly among the depths of life, instead of following the example of the most popular American novelists of the day and lingering in the shallows."

Leaving Hetty to explore her own fantasies, Helen confronted life as it was. She would soon be fifty; and measuring that age against Will's, Helen felt old, her personal and even her professional life stale and meaningless. "I feel isolated in Colorado and cut off from contacts with literary friends," she admitted in a letter to Higginson.

Then an invitation. She was asked to join in a celebration honoring Oliver Wendell Holmes's seventieth birthday. Included in the festivities would be the reading of one of her poems. Again there was the hope that her problems would be solved by a change of scene. A trip east, old friends, new faces and places — she rationalized the possible advantages without an inkling of the real change that awaited her.

Helen was born, twice married, and once widowed in October; the month held a special significance for her. Once again she was destined for a rite of passage — one so startling, so profound, that it would change the course of her life. It occurred curiously enough at a reception honoring some crusading Indians.

During her California trip, Helen had thought the Indians picturesque, had written of "scarlet legs gleaming through the sage," but there'd been other adjectives as well — "abject" and even "loathsome." The two Indians who addressed the assembled group on October 29, 1879, had a sad tale to tell, but they were certainly not abject. Standing Bear, who appealed to the Father in Washington, the Great Spirit, and his White Brothers, was a finely built man well over six feet tall. His niece, Bright Eyes, who translated for him was beautiful by anybody's standards. Both were described later as "picture book Indians." The purpose of their tour was to acquaint the public with the government's systematic extermination of the Ponca Indians of Nebraska.

Helen listened intently as Bright Eyes explained how on three occasions the Poncas had been deprived of their rightful lands. Speaking for Standing Bear, she told of his most recent ordeal: "The soldiers collected all the chiefs together in counsel; and then they took wagons and went round and broke open the houses. When we came back from the council we found the women and children surrounded by a guard of soldiers.

"They took our reapers, mowers, hay-rakes, spades, ploughs, bedsteads, stoves, cupboards, everything we had on our farms and put them in one large building. Then they put into the wagons such things as they could carry. We told them that we would rather die than leave our lands; but we could not help ourselves. They took us down. Many died on the road. Two of my children died. The water was very bad. All our cattle died; not one was left. I stayed till one hundred and fifty-eight of my people had died. Then I ran away with thirty of my people, men and women and children. Some of the children were orphans. We were three months on the road. We were weak and sick and starved. When we reached the Omaha Reserve the Omahas gave us a piece of land, and we were in a hurry to plough it and put in wheat. While we were working the soldiers came and arrested us. Half of us were sick. We would rather have died than have been carried back; but we could not help ourselves."

At gunpoint they had been forced back onto the barren Nebraska sand hills, a totally arid region where nothing could grow and where the last of their horses had quickly died of starvation. Finally the Poncas had taken their case to court, but while the suit dragged on, many were dying of malnutrition. The case was one of civil rights and individual land reforms, but the immediate need was for money and food.

Always with Helen it had come down to a matter of individuals. Continued doubts about Negro equality and feminism never prevented her from cherishing warm friendships among both groups. Never one to involve herself in organized charities, she was invariably warmhearted and generous to anyone who approached her directly. Again and again preconceived beliefs had been tempered or swept aside entirely by the charm or need of an individual. Bright, attractive, needy, Standing Bear and Bright Eyes appealed to Helen, and she immediately determined to help them.

But this time it was different, much more than a kindly whim. For once the urge to do something, to actually make a difference, went beyond the individual. For the first time Helen Hunt Jackson was a woman with a cause.

She would never be the same.

CHAPTER SEVEN

A Lawyer's Brief

Helen's letter shocked him: "I have done now the last of the things I had said I would never do; I have become what I have said a thousand times was the most odious thing in life, 'a woman with a hobby.' But I cannot help it. I think I feel as you must have felt in the old abolition days."

Thomas Higginson responded immediately with an invitation. He'd built a little Queen Anne cottage in Cambridge that he described to Helen as "the ugliest house on Buckingham Street." She went there hoping to secure his active support for her cause. Higginson listened politely and thoughtfully, offering a few experience-based suggestions, but remained detached. The excitement and emotional involvement she'd anticipated weren't there. When the subject had finally run its course, Higginson brought out his little daughter, Margaret Waldo, and introduced her to Helen.

Watching the animated play of expression on the adoring father's face as he described how quickly little Margaret had learned to walk and talk, how responsive she was to picture books and flowers, and so on, Helen understood the sentiments that had replaced political activism. She recalled so well the miraculous freshness of a child's world and felt a double loss.

Helen wasted no time indulging in might-have-beens. Her sudden enthusiasm for her "hobby" had the fervor and obsessive quality of a religious conversion. She had become quite literally a holy terror, bombarding editors with letters and articles, circulating petitions and tracts, raising money for the Ponca's forthcoming lawsuit against the government, and finally declaring open war on Secretary of the Interior Carl Schurz.

When Schurz condescendingly pointed out to her that the lawsuit fund was a waste since the Indians had no legal right to sue either the state or national governments, she attempted to empower these nonpersons by forming the Boston Indian Citizenship Association. It wasn't enough. A broader audience was needed, and Helen decided to marshal all her forces in a book. She would make it "simple and *curtly* a record of our Broken Treaties — and call it *A Century of Dishonor.*"

With each day adding to the list of victimized Indians, Helen could not allow time for a complete history of all the tribes. Her work would be essentially a compilation of raw facts and figures. She settled down in New York, returning day after day to the small alcove assigned to her at the Astor Library, where she read and catalogued every document, every bit of testimony, compiling a grim record of fraud, pillage, oppression, and the worst kind of cruelty. Her first chapter was a sort of lawyer's brief, which she read to two critical attorneys who assured her that it was "strong" and "without a waste word in it."

Helen then presented her case by means of a detailed account of seven tribes followed by exhibits, excerpts from reports, testimonials of Indian character, accounts of outrages committed on Indians by whites, digests of treaties, and a summary of the numbers, locations, and social and economic conditions of every major band of Indians within the country. "I have put an enormous amount of solid work in it," she told Higginson, "& all the heart & soul I possess." Though still removed from the cause, Higginson once again served as her conscientious proofreader; the words and sentiment remained completely her own.

In her conclusion Helen wrote: "It makes little difference where one opens the record of the history of the

Indians; every page and every year has its dark stain. The story of one tribe is the story of all, varied only by differences of time and place; but neither time nor place makes any difference in the main facts. Colorado is as greedy and unjust in 1880 as was Georgia in 1830, and Ohio in 1795; and the United States Government breaks promises now as deftly as then, and with an added ingenuity from long practice."

She reminded her readers that in 1869 President Grant had appointed a commission to investigate the Indian question. The report, which had until now gathered dust on a shelf, had been uniformly in favor of the Indians. "The history of the government connections with the Indians is a shameful record of broken treaties and unfulfilled promises," it began. "The history of the border white man's connection with the Indians is a sickening record of murder, outrage, robbery and wrongs committed by the former, as the rule, and occasional savage outbreaks and unspeakably barbarous deeds of retaliation by the latter, as the exception. . . .

"The testimony of some of the highest military officers of the United States is on record to the effect that, in our Indian wars, almost without exception, the first aggressions have been made by the white man; and the assertion is supported by every civilian of reputation who has studied the subject. In addition to the class of robbers and outlaws who find impunity in their nefarious pursuits on the frontiers, there is a large class of professedly reputable men who use every means in their power to bring on Indian wars for the sake of the profit to be realized from the presence of troops and the expenditures of Government funds in their midst."

Helen's determination grew. Upon publication of *A Century of Dishonor*, a 342-page tract, she sent a copy at her own expense to every member of Congress. Printed in red on the cover were the words of Benjamin Franklin: "Look upon your hands! They are stained with the blood of your relations."

Later—many years later—*A Century of Dishonor* would be referred to as a "watershed book," after it, everything flowing in favor of the Indians. But in January 1881 the immediate outcry of righteous indignation that Helen had hoped to provoke was not forthcoming. Both the public and private sector remained silent; Congress was unmoved.

When reaction finally did come, it was negative. If Helen thought Higginson's response to her enthusiasm was disappointing, Will's was disastrous. After months of separation, he arrived in New York determined to persuade her to give up the crusade and come home.

Had she complied, her welcome would have been anything but warm. Recently an Indian agent had attempted to force the Utes to dig up their sacred dance grounds. Violence had erupted, and he'd been killed. Now Colorado was literally up in arms against the Indians. Soldiers had been called out to defend the residents against anticipated attacks. It was a case of misunderstanding and overreaction, but people were angry, and many of the older inhabitants remembered the violence of the early days, conveniently forgetting that this was the Indians' desperate defense of their own land.

Not only were Colorado residents angry with the Indians, they became furious with Helen for focusing national attention on the embarrassing matter of the Sand Hill Massacre. Twelve years earlier, Colorado Indians had been persuaded to settle in the Sand Hill area by Major E. W. Wynkoop of the First Colorado Cavalry, who promised them provisions and safety. In exchange for this new security, they were encouraged to surrender their arms. A few weeks later, for no apparent reason, they had been attacked in the early dawn hours by a regiment led by Colonel J. M. Chivington of the First Colorado Cavalry—a man Helen later identified as an active member of the Methodist Episcopal Church in Denver.

As the soldiers approached, White Antelope, an Indian chief known to be friendly always to the whites, came running toward them holding up his hands and crying "Stop! Stop!" in English. When he realized that there was no mistake, that the attack was deliberate, he folded his arms and waited calmly for execution. An American flag had been given to the Indians shortly after their arrival, along with a smaller white flag that was offered them by army officials as an additional security. Both pieces of material continued to fly in the breeze above the main lodge of the Indians as eight hundred men, women, and children were slaughtered by the army.

In Denver news of the event had been cause for jubilation. "All have acquitted themselves well," the *Denver News* proclaimed. "Colorado soldiers have again covered themselves with glory." Helen's account described Denver's conquering heroes as "the Colorado regiment of devils."

The former editor of the *Rocky Mountain News,* William N. Byers, took issue. He defended the Interior Department in a letter to the *New York Tribune* and bitterly denounced Helen, who had already sacrificed the esteem of most of her Colorado Springs neighbors. One can only speculate on the effect of her words and actions on Will, whose railroad interests sometimes conflicted with those of the Indians. Continuing to use the newspapers as a public forum, Helen angrily replied to Byers: "That men, exasperated by atrocities and outrages, should have avenged themselves with hot haste and cruelty, was, perhaps, only human; but that men should be found, fifteen years later, apologizing for, nay, justifying the cruel deed, is indeed a matter of marvel."

Then in case anyone should wonder just how cruel the deed was she returned his charges, quoting chapter and verse from sworn and signed statements from the Indian Bureau and the United States Army officers serving in Colorado during the time of the massacre. Included was an account by Major Wynkoop, who was distraught by the repercussions of his original invitation. "Women and children were killed and scalped, children slaughtered at their mothers' breasts, and all the bodies mutilated in the most horrible manner," he said. "The female bodies profaned in such a manner that the recital is sickening, Colonel J. M. Chivington all the time inciting his troops to their diabolical rages."

Robert Bent testified: "I saw a squaw lying on the bank whose leg had been broken. A soldier came up to her with a drawn sabre. She raised her arm to protect herself; he struck, breaking her arm. She rolled over, and raised her other arm; he struck, breaking that, and then left without killing her. I saw one squaw cut open, with an unborn child by her side."

And finally Major Anthony's description: "There was a little child, probably three years old, just big enough to walk through the sand. The Indians had gone ahead, and this little child was behind following them. I saw one man get off his horse at a distance of about seventy-five yards and draw up his rifle and fire. He missed the child. Another man came up and said, 'Let me try the son of a b——. I can hit him.' He got down off his horse, kneeled down, and fired at the little child, but he missed him. A third man came up, and made a similar remark, fired, and the little fellow dropped."

Such graphic accounts may have opened a few eyes in Washington, but did nothing for Helen's popularity in Colorado. Carlyle C. Davis, editor of several Colorado newspapers, who would some thirty years later write a laudatory book, *The True Story of Ramona,* recalled that she was at that time "without a genuine sympathizer in the entire state." This, he regretfully admitted in 1914, included himself — until the onset of Helen's crusade, a close personal friend.

Her compensation came from other sources. On March 3, 1881, Congress passed a bill enabling each individual Ponca to choose the land he preferred, either in the territory tract or on the Niobara, reimbursing each one for his losses and providing funds for houses, schools, and teachers' pay. It was a beginning, but Helen wanted far more. She demanded fair treatment for all the Indians.

Helen was delighted when Jeanette and Joseph Gilder announced that they had a new novel they wanted reviewed for their magazine, *Critic*. The book, *Ploughed Under,* was a story of injustice to the Indians written by her friend William Justin Harsha of the Omaha Ponca Committee. The review proved unexpectedly difficult. Helen liked the author and applauded his subject matter, but found the writing disappointing. The review was tactfully couched. She wanted the novel to be read by a discerning public who would get the message; but as a successful writer and astute editor, she knew it would never do for the Indians what *Uncle Tom's Cabin* had accomplished for the blacks. When she confided her fears to Joseph Gilder, he voiced the thought that had been nagging at her conscience, "You're the one who should tell the story of the Indians, Helen."

"I haven't the time," she informed him firmly. "I lack the background for such a novel. It would take ten years to acquire the local color alone."

"Then take ten years," he persisted.

"When you're as old as I am you won't speak so lightly of ten years," she crisply informed him, putting an end to the subject. Still, the idea was a spark that continued to smolder. She'd been wanting to return to California for nearly ten years. There was so much to see there, the missions to study and write about — surely at fifty she wasn't too old for that. On an impulse she wrote to Will, urging him to make the trip to California with her. She hoped it would be a kind of reconciliation, an opportunity to get to know one another again after so many separations.

She waited eagerly for his answer. It came almost by return mail. He would meet her in Trinidad, Colorado, on April 7 and continue on with her, "treating" himself to the Far West.

Then came an exciting opportunity that neatly dove-tailed. Happily Helen announced to her friend Charles Dudley Warner, editor of the *Hartford Courant:* "We are going to Southern California in two weeks—for a two month trip—Don't you envy us the Sun and flow-ers? I am going to write four articles for Harpers Mags. which is to pay for the luxuries of the trip!" At last it seemed that everything that mattered in Helen's life was coming together: the cause, the career, the man she loved. The contentment she'd longed for suddenly seemed within her grasp.

It wasn't to be. At ten on April 2, 1881, the morning of her departure, a knock at the door interrupted Helen's last-minute packing. It was a telegram from Will. Busi-ness complications forced him to remain in Colorado; he expected her to join him there as soon as possible. She stared at the telegram in disbelief.

Hours later her small suite at the Berkeley still looked like the waiting room at a railroad depot, even to the lunch basket unopened on the sideboard. She sat down to express her frustrations in a note to Warner: "I have been engaged," she told him, "in wild telegraphing back and forth to Mr. Jackson. . . . I am sitting—too mad to unpack—too restless to work—and generally de-moralized—nothing I can think of I want to do except spend money & I've spent money, all I've got. . . ."

She wrote *Harper's Monthly* asking for an extension, but the series was assigned instead to someone else. The disappointment was stunning. Helen wrote again to Warner, complaining that she felt "generally demoral-ized." After her signature, Helen Jackson, she added angrily, "if that's my name, I'm not sure."

Helen stayed on at the Berkeley for a few weeks in a state of rebellion, but by June she had returned to Will and Colorado. It was a lonely summer. Will, engrossed in his own multifaceted business pursuits, had little understanding of Helen's disappointment. If he offered her an apology for his summary dismissal of their plans, it went unrecorded. Helen tried to put the Indians out of her mind. Briefly she traveled with Will to New Mexico, took a few short trips alone, but spent most of her time writing. Another Saxe Holm novel was completed that summer and a small children's book. Colorado Springs had grown to be a city of some forty-five thousand people, but Helen had little contact with any of them. Residents were aloof if not overtly hostile.

In September when Richard Watson Gilder asked her to do a series on the California missions for *Century* Magazine, she was more than ready. With Will, or without him, she was going to California.

CHAPTER EIGHT

A Time Trip

Both modest and majestic, the twenty-one missions, strung like the beads of Father Serra's rosary along the Franciscan friar's Camino Real, are more than just churches, more than mere historic buildings. They are the string tied around the finger of California history.

Confronting a state where old reveries had been transformed overnight into raw newness, Helen perceived them as repositories of common consciousness. Her eastern provincialism was jolted by the realization that these edifices were standing when the Declaration of Independence was signed. She recognized the folk art adaptations of Moorish and Renaissance architecture that the early friars had carried to the new world in their memories and was charmed.

The spawn of generations of rigid Calvinists, her prejudices extended to the point of regarding the Pope as a variety of Anti-Christ, yet within the mission walls, Helen was enveloped by a kind of peace. More significantly, she recognized a fragile fragment of the past, carefully walled in by adobe — a treasure trove of the history she sought to recapture.

Helen saw it all from one perspective — her own. With characteristic enthusiasm, she envisioned eager grateful Indians kneeling dutifully before saintly priests to receive the baptism of a superior culture. She knew that since the seizing of California by the Americans, the California Indian population had dropped significantly, but ignored the larger picture: under the original mission system the statewide Indian population fell from 135,000 in 1770 to 100,000 in 1823 to 73,000 in 1851.

Enveloped by nostalgia for the old missions, which were by the time of Helen's visit in 1881 in total collapse, she deified their founder, Father Junípero Serra, in her *Century* articles as a kind of saint-as-pioneer. Before she was through Helen would visit each mission from San Diego to Sonoma and spend endless hours in the Santa Barbara mission archives — the most complete collection of California Franciscan lore then in existence — as well as in the great historical collection of H. H. Bancroft. The net result of these efforts was the crystallization of her initial reaction. Already for her — and later largely because of her — the mission system shimmered in a golden haze, half memory, half myth.

Even contemporaries had been critical of Serra's not-so,benevolent dictatorship. In 1783 Pedro Fages, military commander of Alta California, had condemned the excessive flogging of the natives for relatively minor indiscretions, writing, "Chastisement by putting in chains was very frequent in all the missions, but principally in Carmel [Serra's primary headquarters]." Later Bancroft, the dean of nineteenth-century-California historians, had described the founding father as "kind hearted and charitable to all, but most strict in his religious duties. It never occurred to him to doubt his absolute right to flog his neophytes in matters of faith."

No matter that the Spanish soldiers hunted down the Indians like so many cattle, or that once in churchly captivity they died. Whether from syphilis contracted from the soldiers, alien work forced on them by the padres, or sheer trauma from being torn from their ancestral homes and stripped of their ancient culture, the consequences remained the same. Helen chose to look beyond all this, focusing instead on intent. What impressed her was the difference in attitude between the Spanish authorities and the Anglo ones. Fresh from her labors in the Astor Library, where she'd seen volumes of evidence bearing out the prevalent American view that the only good Indian was a dead one, she could appreciate the fact that, after all, Serra and the other missionaries hadn't set out deliberately to kill Indians. Far from being the nonpersons viewed by Schurz and the others in the United States Interior Department, as nothing more than troublesome animals to be exterminated, the conquistadors and padres had perceived them as valuable commodities with souls to save and bodies to work. If the grand plan sometimes resulted in death, it was still for the Indians' own good.

Helen had arrived in California in late December, having gone first to New York, where she did additional research on the California Indians at the Astor Library while arming herself for the trip with letters of introduction. This time the transcontinental rendezvous with Will had taken place as planned. They spent all of two days together in Santa Fe, New Mexico, before he went south to El Paso on railroad business and she continued west.

On December 21, 1881, Helen registered at the Pico House in Los Angeles. The hotel, built by Pío Pico, the last Mexican governor of California, was considered the finest in the Southwest. It was the first three-story building in the city and had eighty rooms built Spanish style around a pretty courtyard. Facing as it did on the old plaza, the Pico House gave Helen an ideal vantage point from which to study the one-hundred-year-old town with "its certain indefinable delicious aroma from the old, ignorant, picturesque times."

El Pueblo de Nuestra Señora la Reina de Los Angeles (The Town of Our Lady the Queen of the Angels) was metamorphosing before her very eyes from a sleepy Mexican village to a bustling American city that would within the month announce the introduction of electric street lights and a few cement sidewalks. An influx of easterners had swollen the population to twelve thousand, but the atmosphere was still decidedly Latin.

"This is the picturesque side of the continent," Helen wrote in one of her early articles, "red tiles, brown faces, shawls over heads — dark eyes and soft voices, and the Spanish tongue. . . ." Los Angeles was like a foreign city, still carrying the aura of another time, strange, exotic, its secrets inviolate. She loved the place on sight for those very reasons, but warned others: "Nor, will anyone ever know more of Los Angeles than its lovely outward semblances and mysterious suggestions, unless he have the good fortune to win past the barriers of the proud, sensitive, tender reserve behind which is hid the life of the few remaining survivors of the old Spanish and Mexican regime."

Helen had insured just such good fortune with her letters of introduction and immediately put them to use. One was to the Right Reverend Francis Mora, bishop of Monterey and Los Angeles, who in turn provided her entrée to Don Antonio Coronel and his pretty young wife, Mariana. Don Antonio and his parents had come to California as colonists during the Mexican revolt against Spain. The family prospered, taking an active part in Alta California politics. Until the American invaders ousted him, Don Antonio had served the Mexican government as state treasurer. Anticipating resentment, Helen called on the Coronels with some trepidation. She intended to stay for twenty minutes and remained three hours.

It was love at first sight for all concerned. The Coronels were surprised and delighted by Helen; she was charmed and intrigued by them. At their insistence she joined them on Christmas Day and was from then on a frequent guest at El Recreo, the Coronels' stately home surrounded by orchards, orange groves, and vineyards at what is now the northwest corner of Seventh and Alameda streets. She found the place a treasure house, both inviting and elegant, filled with romantic relics of the past. Don Antonio could speak little English, but sang and strummed his guitar for her in the old Spanish manner. At the end of each visit, Helen left with her arms filled with clusters of fruit and flowers and a head full of stories from the old days, which Doña Mariana had translated.

Don Antonio shared Helen's deep concern for the Indians who'd saved his life more than once during the early violence of the American takeover. Now he outlined a travel plan for her that would enable her to visit the last of the old land-grant ranchos as well as see firsthand what had become of the former Mission Indians.

The land monopoly of the mission system had been broken by the Secularization Act instigated by the Mexican government in 1833. By the end of the decade, the Indians had been freed; some had continued to live unmolested on the land they'd once been forced to till. Others, as the mission property was sold, were dispersed but given substitute land by the new private owners. Most of these original Mexican land grants included clauses protecting the Indians on the farms they occupied.

Then in 1846 the Americans arrived and immediately challenged the Californios to produce proof of ownership. It did little good to point out that an old forgotten piece of paper was unnecessary to prove title to land that everyone knew had been in the family for decades — sometimes since the days of the Spanish kings. Ancient families were ruined in a day, empires lost overnight; but the most seriously jeopardized were invariably the Indians. The conquering Americans had a history of ignoring claims. Once again the Indian was a disenfranchised nonperson. Since Indians weren't citizens, it seemed perfectly fair and reasonable to the new white settlers who wanted their lands to certify to the land agent that those lands were "unoccupied." It was the same old story, one more injustice tailor-made for Helen's pencil.

A friend from her early days in Colorado Springs, Flora Haines Apponyi, encountered Helen by chance in Los Angeles and was surprised at the changes a few years had brought. "I remembered her as a charming, brown-haired woman with thoughtful eyes, frank of speech with a merry laugh and a warm heart for those she liked," Flora later recalled in an *Overland* sketch.

That "winsome" woman was gone. "Years of high thought, of deep study and earnest purpose had dignified and ennobled her face and the whitening hair which crowned her broad forehead invested her with a regal air which was borne out by her perfect self poise and commanding decision. This was at the time of her greatest activity, when she prosecuted her work with unresting energy."

In mid-January Helen had followed one of Don Antonio's leads to the Santa Barbara Mission. During the heyday of the system, Santa Barbara had been like the other missions, a self-sustaining feudal community with vast lands devoted to orchards, vineyards, and grain as well as to the pasturing of cattle, sheep, and horses and the quartering of troops. By the time of Helen's visit, the once-vast holdings had dwindled to little more than the mission itself, but unlike the others it hadn't been abandoned or abused. A few of the Franciscan fathers remained and with them a cache of priceless memorabilia gathered from the other missions following secularization.

Helen remained in the area researching for more than a month. During that time she had an opportunity to visit the holdings of Ellwood Cooper. The place was referred to by the locals as a "pocket ranch," for it comprised a mere two thousand acres, but it impressed Helen. She'd been taken to the highest elevation to view the landscape, a colorful collage of wheat fields, orchards in blossom, and olive groves, with the Pacific shimmering in the distance. Perhaps a little of her Puritan background crept unrealized into Helen's *Century* account of all this abundance: "In observing the industries of Southern California one never escapes from an undercurrent of wonder that there should be any industries or industry there. No winter to be prepared for, no fixed time at which anything must be done or not done at all;

the air sunny, palmy, dreamy, seductive, making the mere being alive in it a pleasure; all sorts of fruits and grains growing a-riot, and taking care of themselves — it is easy to understand the character; or to speak more accurately, the lack of character, of the old Mexican and Spanish Californians."

The Santa Fe Railroad hadn't yet linked San Diego to the rest of the state when Helen arrived in that city on March 4, 1882. She came by the side-wheeler *S.S. Oriza-ba* from Santa Barbara. Landing at Horton's Wharf at the foot of Fifth Avenue, she was confronted with what had literally become Horton's town. A visionary and a land developer, Alonzo Horton had come to San Diego in 1867 and had proceeded to totally transform it. Disdainfully surveying the sleepy village now called Old Town, he informed its three hundred and fifty inhabitants, "Never in this world can you have a city here." He proposed as an alternative a whole new city a few miles south, near the bay. Only Horton saw its advantages, but his vision was clear. He quickly bought 960 acres of what would soon be downtown San Diego. By 1870 he'd turned it all into 50-by-100-foot lots that sold so rapidly that San Diego's leading newspaper, *The Union,* had moved its offices to Horton's "New Town."

The pride of this burgeoning metropolis was the Horton House, and it was there that Helen went immediately. The two-story brick building, fronting on the bay on D Street between Third and Fourth, catered "to people of means and taste in San Diego." It boasted sixty-eight rooms, hot and cold running water in nearly every room, and two tin bathtubs. More important to Helen, it offered free transportation to anywhere in the county. She was going to need that.

"A handsome woman with a commanding air," Helen made a lasting impression. One contemporary explained, "She was unsparing of her criticism and was as enthusiastic and earnest when discussing drainage as she was when speaking of art or poetry. The truth is that H. H. was by nature combative. She delighted to expose the wrong, or to lay bare the weak side of men, women, and things. Fearless of criticism herself, she never hesitated to speak her mind no matter who might suffer. As a result the friends she did have were warm ones, and her enemies were true haters. If she liked, she loved; and if she disliked, she despised." Small wonder that more than fifty years later two former clerks recalled how she'd taken the manager to task for his child-rearing skills and startled the other guests by dressing for dinner. The staff thought her eastern expectations a bit "unreasonable."

A writer for the *San Francisco Chronicle* who met Helen about this time told his readers that "she had grown stout recently, and her hair turned quite gray; but she is still very young in feeling and manner, and all her acquaintances pronounce her a charming woman whom her own sex are drawn to, and whom the other sex fall in love with instinctively."

Helen quickly found common interests with a resident in the hotel, Mariette Gregory, a renowned clairvoyant. There's no record of whether or not Mrs. Gregory was able to get through to Rennie in the other world, but she did prove invaluable as an interpreter and resource person in this one. The seer shared Helen's deep concern for the Indians and had traveled freely about the back country, talking with them and gaining their confidence. She told shocking stories of how the Indian women had been taken by force by the white squatters who'd invaded the area.

There were other new friends as well. The Ephraim Moreses, Massachusetts transplants like Helen, took her riding in their carriage out to the tip of Point Loma, a drive she would recall as "the most beautiful in America."

Helen developed many valuable connections in San Diego, but of them all Father Anthony Ubach proved the most valuable. She'd heard of his work among the

Indians and was anxious from the first to interview him. The priest was living in Old Town in the abandoned Casa de Estudillo, a run-down relic of grander days that would one day become a kind of shrine to thousands of tourists seeking "Ramona's marriage place." A cigar-smoking militant with an outspoken tongue and a strong taste for Spanish wine, Ubach couldn't have been more surprised to find himself woven into a sentimental romance; yet he would eventually figure prominently in *Ramona,* appearing as Father Gaspara.

The man who greeted Helen was a soldier-type priest who angrily protested the treatment of the Indians whose responsibility he'd shouldered. He was delighted to find a potential ally in this equally outspoken eastern woman and was happy to drive her about the countryside in his two-horse, double-seated carriage. Helen traveled with him from early morning to late evening, visiting the remnants of missions and locating mission Indians. She attended trials involving Indian offenders, visited pitiful hovels on hills and in canyons where the dispossessed just barely managed to survive. Helen was shocked by the degradation and reluctantly admitted in an article, "Most of these Indians are miserable, worthless beggars, drunkards, of course, and worse."

Ubach told her stories of San Diego and its past. One that left a mark was about a young couple who'd appeared at his door late one night. The woman was the daughter of a prominent Californio family, the man an Indian sheepherder. They begged him to marry them immediately. This he did — not in the Estudillo house where he was living, but in the small adobe Chapel of the Immaculate Conception on Conde Street. Soon after, the couple was apprehended by the bride's angry family. The marriage was annulled, the young woman subsequently forced into marriage with another, the Indian flogged nearly to death. It was tragic, romantic, a tale that Helen would not forget.

Traveling in a northeasterly direction from San Diego, Father Ubach and Helen visited the enchanting valley of San Pasqual, which looked to Helen like one continuous field of wheat. Ubach recalled that when he'd first visited the area fifteen years earlier, he'd found a thriving community of some three hundred Indians. He'd been relieved in 1870 when assurance came from the United States government that they would be allowed to remain on the lands of their fathers.

But this was not to be. Greedy settlers — "robber whites," as Helen called them — fought the ruling, slowly, insidiously encroaching on the San Pasqual Reservation. The Indians had finally been forced to abandon their well-cultivated farms, to leave behind their family homes. The one remaining native was an old man, nearly blind, who was forced by circumstances to work for the very farmers who'd dispossessed him. The rest, Helen was to write, "had fled like wild beasts into secret lairs."

Temecula was even worse. All that remained of the Indians there was their graveyard. This, too, had been ancestral land belonging to what had once been the San Luis Rey Mission Indians. Their claim had been a clear one based on a protective clause in an early Mexican land grant deeding the area back to them. In 1852 the United States government conceded the grant in its Treaty of Peace and Freedom.

The treaty and the "peace and freedom" it guaranteed lasted until 1869 when five white settlers from San Francisco saw the land and instigated legal action to get it for themselves. The Indians had appealed to Father Ubach to intercede for them, and he in turn had appealed to one of the judges in the case. These efforts merely delayed the inevitable. In 1875 the sheriff of San Diego arrived with a posse of determined men and a warrant. This, Helen learned, not only deprived the Indians of their homes and their crops just maturing for harvest, but their personal property was taken in satisfaction of the cost of the settlement.

Helen listened eagerly as Father Ubach talked to the Indians in their various dialects and then translated for her. In this way she learned of an Indian school in Saboba, the first in the state. She was excited by the possibilities of such a facility and prevailed on Ubach to make the seventy-five-mile trip with her. They found a village of one hundred and fifty Indians from the Serrano tribe living in a fertile section of the San Jacinto Valley watered by a natural spring.

Their chief, Jesús Castillo — who in the modern fashion called himself a "captain" — explained that his people had settled on the land more than one hundred years earlier. Looking about at the attractive, well-cared-for homes, the lush fields, vineyards, livestock, and orchards, Helen thought it all too good to be true — and it was.

"The Serranos are in danger of losing their lands," Mary Sheriff, the schoolteacher, announced as they toured the village. She explained how in 1842 the Mexican government had granted most of the San Jacinto Valley to José Antonio Estudillo with the stipulation that he safeguard the security of the Indians living there. The Indians' position had been strengthened further just two years before Helen's visit when the United States government confirmed the original Mexican patent. Through the years Estudillo had been faithful to his promise, and the Indians had thrived unmolested; but now the patriarch was dead, and his many heirs were not so conscientious. Parcels of land were sold at random whenever anyone in the family needed money. One of the new owners, M. R. Byrnes, threatened to evict the Indians unless the United States government agreed to buy his entire seven hundred acres.

The Indian captain, Jesús Castillo, was bewildered and defenseless. "If the Government says we must go, we must; but we would rather die right here than move," he'd told Miss Sheriff.

She in turn confided her fears to Helen, "The Indians may give in without a struggle."

Helen was adamant, "We just can't let them do that."

Mary Sheriff had volunteered for her job, and she loved it. She described the aptitude and charm of her charges in glowing terms. Helen, as always touched by anything having to do with children, was impatient to meet them. To her surprise, their reaction was anything but friendly.

Later Mary would recall the incident: "Mrs. Jackson was then about forty-eight years old. She was fair and blue-eyed with blond hair turning gray which she wore curled about a smooth brow. She was plump but of neat form, weighing about one hundred and fifty pounds and was about five foot, three inches in height. She had beautiful hands, white, firm, shapely and well kept. Hands that could do things well.

"When she came to San Jacinto she wore a gray traveling dress with gray bonnet to match, upon which was the head of a large gray owl, Indian name, tutacote. In our walks about the village, Mrs. Jackson tried to get acquainted with some of the little children but they would scurry out of sight as soon as she approached their homes, only deigning to peek around the corner when I called to them that the lady had dulce (candy) for them. I knew there must be something out of the ordinary the matter when they refused to come for dulce, for they were exceedingly fond of sweets.

"The little ones were in the habit of giving me the Spanish diminutive of 'Mamá,' with them it is a term of endearment. As we passed along the street I heard them calling from their hiding places: 'Mamacita! Mamacita! cita, cita, mirala tutacote un tutacote malas.' (See the owl, the bad owl.) And then I knew what was the matter. The large owl is the Indian bird of ill omen. If it hovers over your head it brings a message of your death, but if it flies toward you it tells of the death of one that is dear to you. One of the mothers told me that the children were greatly distressed. They were afraid the owl might fly over me. When I told Mrs. Jackson, she said, tenderly, 'It is too bad to frighten the poor children. I will not wear it again.'"

Helen removed her owl, thinking the children already had more than enough to be frightened of — if they but knew it. From then on she made friends quickly. Helen became the "good lady": she and her sweets both in much demand. One little girl even begged to go home with her. Helen explained gently but firmly that this was impossible. To herself she acknowledged the truth, she really had no home.

Mary Sherriff later recalled an afternoon when she and Helen, accompanied by Jesús Castillo, had visited the nearby graveyard. "The sight of so many tiny graves touched Mrs. Jackson's mother-heart and when the Captain, in answer to her questions, told how the poor little things suffered during the rainy season for want of warm bedding and clothes to keep them warm, tears came to her eyes."

Later that same day Helen expressed a desire to see the inside of one of the Indian homes. Soon, Mary would remember later, they were knocking at the door of an Indian home near the edge of the bluff. "A young and rather pretty Indian woman invited us to enter. Her baby was ill and she had it in just such a cradle, made from twigs woven together as Mrs. Jackson afterwards described in *Ramona*. The mother said she feared the baby would die. Then with quivering lips, she said, 'We sent to San Bernardino for a doctor to come to the village to see if he could not cure my little one, but he refused. He told my husband to give the medicine he gave him and if she did not get better to bring her to San Bernardino but she is too ill to bear the journey.' Mrs. Jackson's eyes flashed fire as she questioned the woman to make sure the doctor understood how sick the child was when he refused to come."

That night Mary, who was sharing her room with Helen, realized that her guest was wide awake. "I grew uneasy," she recalled, "and asked Mrs. Jackson if she was ill. 'No,' she said, 'but when I close my eyes, I see that poor little suffering baby that might get well if the doctor had a heart.'"Helen thought of the Indians' threatened eviction and of the gentle resignation of Jesús, their captain, and resolved that something must — and would — be done for these people.

By the first week in April, Helen was back in Los Angeles. She settled into the Kimball Mansion on New High Street, preferring its comfort and good food to the more pretentious atmosphere of the Pico House. It proved a lucky choice. One of the first people she met there was Abbot Kinney, a globe-trotting visionary with a warm heart and a lively curiosity. At thirty Kinney had already lost and recouped a major fortune. Plagued by insomnia, he was advised that the "right" climate would cure him. Despite his extensive wanderings, he'd reached San Francisco virtually sleepless and had planned to take the next train east. Severe snowstorms had paralyzed the railroad, and Kinney was forced to delay his homeward journey until the snowpack melted. With time to spare, he decided to visit Southern California. Arriving at the Sierra Madre Inn in the Los Angeles foothills, he found the place filled to capacity and was advised to take temporary shelter in the parlor. After an exhausting game of billiards, Kinney, at last tired, slumped over sound asleep across the gaming table. In the morning he described it as "the best damn night's sleep" he'd ever had. Kinney decided to make his home in the south and had been living there for nearly two years when he and Helen met.

This thirty-two-year-old wunderkind who'd already managed to see much of the world attracted Helen's interest. She liked what she read in the earnest young face half hidden under a thicket of russet hair and a full beard. Kinney's adventurous life appealed to her; he was a kindred spirit with an outspoken sympathy for the Indians that came close to matching her own.

His business in Los Angeles completed, the youthful entrepreneur who would one day found the California city of Venice, invited Helen to visit him at his home in the San Gabriel Mountains. Intrigued as always by novelty, she agreed. In the meantime Helen summarized her California rambles in a letter to her friend William Hayes Ward at the *New York Independent,* "I have had a most interesting winter; a month in Los Angeles — one in Santa Barbara — then in San Diego — Riverside and San Bernardino, and am back in Los Angeles to wait the arrival of the artist who will illustrate my articles."

The wait was pleasant and profitable. She renewed her acquaintance with Jeanne Carr and her husband, Professor Ezra Slocum Carr. She'd met the couple thirty years earlier at a meeting of the American Associaton for the Advancement of Science in Providence. As she and Jeanne described their subsequent life experiences to each other, those early days seemed a world away. At that time the two women had been scarcely more than brides. In the intervening years Carr had left his post at the University of Wisconsin to head the Natural Science and Chemistry Department at the University of California at Berkeley. The aggressive young professor that Helen remembered was retired now. The Carrs intended to settle in Pasadena, where they had bought property.

Helen couldn't help contrasting her life with that of her old friend. Jeanne also had had two sons, but hers had lived. Now they were young men with lives of their own. Jeanne was filling the void with new interests. Her home — a forty-two-acre tract, originally nothing more than a sun-scorched sheep run — stretched from what is now Orange Grove Street on the west to Fair Oaks Avenue on the east and northward from Colorado Street. She had named the place Carmelita (little grove) and was busy transforming a barren plain into a garden sanctuary of trees and flowers.

The two women explored the countryside in a spring wagon driven by Jeanne's young Chinese house servant and pulled by two half-wild broncos. On one occasion Helen surprised them all by crying, "Stop! Stop! Let me out!" The startled driver had barely reined in the horses before Helen, impetuous as ever despite her years, jumped from the wagon. The object of her excitement was a huge clump of yellow mustard.

She ran toward the golden thicket. "Don't speak to me, don't say a word," Jeanne later recalled her saying; and, watching in amazement, she saw her friend whip out a notebook and pencil and begin writing furiously. Later that day Helen recopied and amplified her notes in Dr. Carr's study.

Jeanne remembered that sunny afternoon nostalgically. A few years later she read in *Ramona:* "The wild mustard in Southern California is like that spoken of in the New Testament, in the branches of which the birds of the air may rest. Coming up out of the earth, so slender a stem that dozens can find starting point in an inch, it darts up, a slender straight shoot, five, ten, twenty feet, with hundreds of fine feathery branches, locking and interlocking with all the hundreds around it, till it is an inextricable network of lace. Then it bursts into yellow bloom still finer, more feathery and lace-like. The stems are so infinitesimally small, and of so dark a green, that at a short distance they do not show, and the cloud of blossom seems floating in the air; at times it looks like golden dust. With a clear blue sky behind it, as it is often seen, it looks like a golden snow-storm."

It is against just such a "swaying frame of blossoms" that Helen's immortal heroine was introduced. Very probably recalling that shimmering moment, she would one day write: "Ramona's beauty was of the sort to be best enhanced by the waving gold which now framed her face. She had just enough of olive tint in her complexion to underlie and enrich her skin without making it swarthy. Her hair was like her Indian mother's, heavy and black, but her eyes were like her father's, steel blue. . . ."

Another day that Jeanne wasn't likely to forget was their first visit to Kinneyloa, the mountaintop home of Abbot Kinney. They'd made the trip at Helen's insistence; she'd admired his style in Los Angeles and hoped to know him better. That opinion changed as they climbed higher into the San Gabriel Mountains. Kinneyloa was visible for miles, an eyesore that offended her every sensibility. "Don't say anything to me about that man who could put a great staring white house on a hill like that," she admonished Jeanne.

Higher and higher they climbed, Helen fuming all the while. But when they finally reached the house and Abbot Kinney met them at the door, Helen found herself melting. Kinney *was* charming, just as appealing as she'd remembered; and his home was interesting in a bizarre kind of way. Loa means mountain in Hawaiian, he explained. One of his more recent homes had been in the Sandwich Islands, and he was full of stories about his adventures there. Inside the house were all kinds of treasures culled from his travels and a staff of Chinese servants to keep them dusted. Outside were seventeen cats, maintained to stabilize the gopher population. It was a fascinating afternoon and the beginning of a lifelong friendship.

In May Henry Sandham arrived from the East to begin illustrating Helen's articles. Together they retraced her previous journey to San Diego, to the missions San Luis Rey and San Juan Capistrano, and to numerous Indian villages. At Helen's suggestion — he later complained she was always at his elbow — Sandham made sketches of crumbling chapels and Indian huts, cracked mission bells, and colorful Indian baskets.

Ten days later they were back in Los Angeles. Helen returned to the Kimball Mansion and arranged for her illustrator to stay with the Coronels. She wanted Sandham to soak up atmosphere while listening to a few of Don Antonio's California tales.

From there they were to go north; and, whatever his preferences in houses, Helen wanted Abbot Kinney along. Not only did he like Indians, he was beginning to speak their language. Without too much effort, she persuaded him to accompany them.

The trio sailed May 21 for Santa Barbara. After a few days of additional fact finding for Helen and sketching for Sandham, they continued northward to San Luis Obispo, Paso Robles, Mission San Antonio de Padua and Jolon. It was a sizzling hot trip by carriage and wagon over rough, bumpy roads. Helen's nerves were grayed by the time they reached San Juan Bautista. She was pleased by the place that she later described in a *Century* article as having "sun, valley, and seaward outlook, unsurpassed in all California," but quarreled with the parish father, Valentine Closa. Outspoken as ever, she took the priest to task for neglecting the needs of the Indians who remained in the area. A hot-tempered Spanish Moor, Closa resented her criticism and said so. His job was to save the souls of the Indians, their bodies were their own responsibility. Helen left, some say, "in anger."

A telegram from Will awaited her in Monterey. He was en route to California and wanted her to meet him at the Palace Hotel in San Francisco. From there they would sail to Oregon, Puget Sound, and Vancouver. To Helen in her stifling hotel room, the message seemed heaven-sent. A conciliatory Will . . . the sea voyage . . . best of all, it would be *cool*. She was waiting for him at the Palace.

The holiday was the happiest kind, a physical and emotional renewal. And, as always, it provided a subject for Helen's busy pencil. In an article, "Chance Days in Oregon," she wrote, "Our recollections of the journey are still mingled with that sort of exultant sense of delight with which the human mind always regards a purely fortuitous possession."

Will urged her to return with him by rail to Colorado Springs. "There's no reason why you can't write your stories back home with me instead of alone in Los Angeles," he pointed out. Helen agreed. There really wasn't — just as long as Will realized that she had no intention of giving up her crusade.

Helen had become familiar with ranch life, missions, and reservations. She had used her superb reportorial skill to absorb facts and figures as well as atmosphere. She possessed vision, imagination, and stamina — the requisite equipment to write a great novel.

All she lacked was the story.

CHAPTER NINE

A Junketing Female Commissioner

Ralph Waldo Emerson had called Helen "America's greatest poet"; but with *A Century of Dishonor,* she'd forsaken the muse along with her precious anonymity. The tract had been a savage attack, her pencil a crusader's lance tearing relentlessly at the vulnerability of a flaccid, frequently corrupt government.

Back again in Colorado Springs, she readied herself for another assault. Awaiting her return was a letter from Mary Sheriff. Though M. R. Byrnes had originally purchased his land from the Estudillo heirs with the stipulation that he use it only for sheep grazing—leaving the area occupied by the Saboba Indians inviolate—he had recently announced his intention to have them evicted unless the government agreed to buy the entire tract from him for thirty thousand dollars. At first distraught by the news, Helen strengthened her resolve. If the Indians were to be saved, it was she who would have to do it. She determined to return again to California; but this time with the authority to effect changes.

Helen immediately fired off a letter to Secretary of the Interior Henry Teller, warning: "There is grave danger of continued Indian massacres. If the United States Government does not take steps to avert this danger, the chapter of the Mission Indians will be the blackest one in the record of our dealings with the Indian race."

She appealed to Teller because they'd met once in Denver when the politician had been briefly associated with Will. Writing back to Mary, Helen offered what little encouragement she could, explaining that she'd "told him all about the positions of these Indians here in S. Cal. and the certainty that they will be driven off every one of their homesteads in a few years if the Govt. does not protect them." Doubt and frustration were apparent in her closing, "I hope something will come of the letter." When nothing did, she wrote Teller again on June 11, 1882. This time she enclosed a pleading note from Jesús, the Saboba captain. Teller promised to take the matter under advisement.

Skeptical of promises, Helen then applied to Commissioner of Indian Affairs Hiram Price. She was seeking a government appointment to serve as a one-woman fact-finding committee. "My own expenses I will rate, as I told Mr. Teller, at twelve hundred dollars," she explained. "If it takes longer and costs more, I will defray the remainder myself."

Helen's proposal was clear. She would report directly to the Interior Department concerning: (1) the present number of Indians living in Southern California and their living conditions, (2) the amount of government land available to them, (3) the possibility of other areas that might be purchased for the Indians in the absence of government land, and (4) the Indians' own feelings about being moved to reservations.

Teller and Price were impressed by the plan, sufficiently impressed for the latter to recommend that she be designated Special Commissioner of Indian Affairs in Southern California — the first woman to hold that position. President Chester Arthur approved the measure on July 7, 1882.

Helen had once advised her sometime friend, feminist Kate Field: "Never have a hobby. If you do, it will ride you to death." Following her appointment, Kate called her to account: "Who has the hobby now? What are the Indians to you, that you are working yourself to death in their behalf?"

Acknowledging her reversal with a shrug, Helen replied: "I used to imagine that I was a woman who would never change her mind. As I grow older I discover myself to be one who will not mind in the least what she thought or said yesterday, provided today she finds she was mistaken. I have a hobby now, and only wish I had the power to ride it to victory."

Writing to her longtime friend and confidant Charles Dudley Warner, Helen admitted that she was no "saner" on the Indian question than before and that "there is not in all the Century of Dishonor, so black a chapter as the history of the Mission Indians — venerable farmers for a hundred years — driven off their lands like foxes and wolves — driven *out* of good adobe houses and the white men who had driven them out sitting down calm and comfortable in the homes!" But she was jubilant about her appointment. Other agents had reported on the conditions of the Indians, but Helen was certain that she could do it better. She would write an account that would change minds by "reaching hearts." It would also, she decided, reach the pages of the *New York Independent*.

When the elation of winning her first round with the government subsided a bit, the enormity of it all became apparent, and she was confronted with the fact that the task was too vast for her to accomplish alone. What she needed was an associate, someone to interface with the Indians. Abbot Kinney came immediately to mind. He not only had a working knowledge of their language, but also understood and sympathized with their culture. Equally important, he was conversant with California land laws.

Helen immediately wrote Price requesting that Kinney be appointed her coagent and interpreter. His response was negative, so she appealed once more to Teller for support. When none came, she was temporarily stalemated. Helen had made her point to the government. Both Price and Teller had at last accepted the truth in her statements, the merit of her cause. Now, she hoped, they would yield to her in the matter of Kinney as well. She considered him absolutely essential to the successful completion of her mission; and, as in her dealings with editors, Helen recognized when to stand her ground.

In the meantime there was plenty to keep her busy. The most important effort of the summer was the writing of her California series for *Century*. Richard Gilder wanted a "popular treatment"; Helen had a message to impart. It was a challenge to reconcile the two. Yet interspersed with the articles she tossed off a quick series of poems, essays, and a short book, *The Training of Children*, for Roberts Brothers — its theme gentle reason in lieu of corporeal punishment.

When the *Century* series was completed, Will suggested a trip to Mexico. Helen eagerly agreed, and at dusk on the evening of September 27, they boarded the Thunderbolt, the Atchison, Topeka & Santa Fe's newest record-breaking addition. On September 29 they watched the sun come up while breakfasting in El Paso. Across the Rio Grande Helen could see Paso del Norte, (now Juárez) Mexico, "an almost unbroken line of mud houses." It was a thrilling experience. "A few years ago," the seasoned travel writer recorded for her readers, "to have spoken of running down from Colorado to the Mexican boundary for a few days' trip would have been preposterous, yet to do so today is only a matter of thirty-six hours."

She was less enthusiastic about the relic of the old Butterfield Stage Line that took them across the river, "antiquated, ragged . . . with seats of bare boards"; but once on the other side, she marveled at the three-hundred-year-old town: "To be here on Sunday is to escape from America and the nineteenth century."

Their whirlwind visit was marred somewhat by Helen's impatience. She had expected to find confirmation of Kinney's appointment waiting for her back in Colorado Springs, but was surprised and disappointed by continued governmental silence. She hadn't anticipated so long a wait. The impasse was turning into a war of nerves, but Helen wasn't about to give in—far too much was at stake. Hoping to make the time pass faster, she decided to go to New York to deliver her California articles to Gilder in person; and because they were so very important, she would get Higginson's reaction first.

Once again Higginson welcomed her to his Queen Anne cottage in Cambridge. As in the old days, Helen sat anxiously at her mentor's side while he scrutinized each word. At last he returned the articles to her. He was "moderately satisfied," but suggested a few significant changes. Helen settled down in Boston to do rewrites. She wanted desperately to sway public opinion with her words and hoped to appeal to "minds comparatively uninformed about the subject." With this objective, she appealed to friends to serve as devil's advocates, to listen critically as she read her articles aloud to them.

Satisfied at last, Helen submitted her series to Gilder. She was immensely relieved by his enthusiastic response, but would have been flabbergasted could she have known the ultimate success of the articles, that they would be assembled in book form twenty years later as *Glimpses of California and the Missions,* the definitive early-twentieth-century travel guide to Southern California.

There'd been talk of Will's joining her in the East in December, but Christmas came and went without him. Then on January 12, 1883, the Interior Department informed her of Abbot Kinney's confirmation as her coagent. Helen was on her way to California without even a stop in Colorado Springs.

Leaving behind snow, sleet, hail, city grime, and soot, she stepped off the train seven days later to find "a pot of gold." To Helen's eager eyes it was "a miraculous sight." Soon a euphoric article appeared in the *Independent* describing willows, flowers, square miles of orange orchards, and "everyone outdoors as though it were midsummer." Exaggeration possibly, but Helen was her ardent self again after what had to her seemed months of forced inactivity.

Kinney found her enthusiasm contagious. Jokingly, he referred to Helen as "the general," for she was definitely in charge. She called him Comrade, which was quickly shortened to Co. The talented illustrator, Henry Sandham, who reluctantly joined them — grumbling all the way — was always Henry.

The party bounced along the byways of Southern California in a carriage driven by Newell Mitchell, the proprietor of an Anaheim livery stable. Following old stagecoach routes, they visited reservation after reservation, Kinney digging for details, Sandham sketching, and Helen tirelessly writing, recording for her passionate indictment names, fact, figures. On two occasions they arrived just in time to intercede for San Ysidro Indians at the very moment when white squatters were attempting to seize their land. Helen was especially grateful to Abbot then; his authoritative charisma, tall, imposing presence, and unfailing sense of humor had become indispensable. How right she'd been to stand firm against the government regarding his appointment.

As they ascended the mountainous approach to Julian, located in the San Ysidro Valley, which had been until that moment basking in the spring sunshine, they were suddenly caught in a freak snowstorm. It was an experience that Helen would remember always. Later, recapturing the ordeal in *Ramona*, she would write: "A fierce wind blew from the north, and tearing off the fleeces from the black clouds, sent them in scurrying masses across the sky. In a moment more, snow-flakes began to fall. . . . Still thicker and faster fell the snow; the air was dense; it was worse than the darkness of night, — this strange opaque whiteness, thick, choking, freezing one's breath. Presently the rough jolting of the wagon showed that we were off the road. The horses stopped; refused to go."

Helen's party was able to take shelter in an abandoned shack where they were virtually imprisoned for three days while the storm beat down upon them, penetrating the cracks in the wall. Again she would incorporate the experience in *Ramona*: "The place which at first seemed a haven of warmth, was indeed but a poor shelter against the fearful storm that raged outside. It was only a hut of rough boards, carelessly knocked together for a shepherd's temporary home. It had been long unused, and many of the boards were loose and broken. Through these crevices, at every blast of the wind, the fine snow swirled."

When the storm showed no sign of abating and they could stand the cold and hunger no longer, Mitchell proposed a daring plan. He would drive into the teeth of the gale. Staggering out into the blizzard, Mitchell somewhat managed to harness the horses. Helen, Abbot, and Henry floundered their way to the wagon and climbed in. Cracking his whip, praying, and cursing, the driver guided them through the whirling snowdrifts to safety.

Although that was the most harrowing experience, none of the trip was easy. Helen's self-imposed assignments took them to seemingly endless deserts and bleak mountain passes, areas so hazardous that they had to abandon their wagon for burros, the only creature sure-footed enough to negotiate the precipitous trails. Often Henry remonstrated with Helen — it was too difficult, too dangerous for a woman, particularly at her age. Perhaps he hoped that if she gave up, he could as well; if so, the strategy didn't work. Helen was openly scornful; it was usually Henry who tired the fastest and complained the most. "I'll go if it kills me," she frequently challenged him.

The always-stylish Helen seems to have adapted remarkably well to her environment and circumstances. A friend meeting her at this time remarked on Helen's "dainty neatness and the sense of fitness which led her to choose without wasting much thought upon it, what was becoming and best suited to her style." (One wonders what Helen chose for sleeping in haystacks, which she did upon occasion.) Her hair was cut short now,

"growing in soft rings like a baby's round her face."
The effect was to make her "seem always young" and
must have made wilderness travel easier to cope with.
More important, Co and the driver, N. H. Mitchell,
thought her a "companion of companions." Mitchell
years later recalled Helen as "smiling, good natured,
witty, but always earnest and determined."

Returning from the wild interior lands, Helen was
more amused than annoyed to learn that her travels had
been publicized and that she was referred to as a "junketing female commissioner." The charge, with its free-
loading connotations, was absurd to anyone with any
awareness of the true circumstances of her hazardous
backcountry expeditions. She was far more concerned by
the lack of sympathy for the cause itself.

Helen's tireless travels weren't likely to win her any
medals from the locals, many of whom were outraged by
her defense of the Indians. *A Century of Dishonor* hadn't
been received with any more enthusiasm in California
than it had in Colorado. To the Californios, Helen was
merely one more meddling easterner, an officious newcomer to be scorned, while the settlers, recognizing her as
a threat to their newly acquired estates, greeted her with
open hostility.

The establishment press withheld judgment. On April
6, 1883, the *Los Angeles Express* reported, "The lady is
a comparative stranger and what she possesses in the
way of qualifications for this responsible position will
have to be shown by such action as she may see fit to
take in this matter."

By that time Helen had established herself temporarily
at Mrs. E. W. Whipple's boardinghouse on Tenth and G
streets in San Diego, a place she called "the best of all
possible towns." Helen had a bright, airy second-floor
room with an attractive southern exposure; and, as
always, she found a little time to indulge her flair for
interior design. The other Whipple residents watched
with interest as her room quickly filled with "pretty
things" she had acquired on her fact-finding excursions.

She was an avid collector and could never see something beautiful without longing to possess it. Now Helen had a double motive for displaying her colorful acquisitions. She hoped that by demonstrating the artistry of the native baskets and embroidery she could help to reveal the Indian culture to skeptical Anglos.

Another Whipple resident, Margaret Allen, remembered that Helen "made a most delightful addition to the family." That "family" was made up for the most part of railroad officials, army officers and their wives, a smattering of tourists, and a few schoolteachers. Years later, many of the residents vividly recalled the visiting writer, whom they described as "handsome, self-possessed and spontaneous." A few would have preferred a more cautious spontaneity.

One resident was a schoolteacher who frequently regaled the dinner guests around the boardinghouse table with critical accounts of the "imps" she was supposed to instruct. She very clearly disliked both the children and teaching — or so it appeared to Helen, whose sympathy for the students increased with each evening's discourse.

At one memorable dinner, the teacher gave yet another witty monologue at the expense of a pupil. Helen could stand it no longer. Her eyes flashing, she came to the defense of the absent child. "I wonder that the board allows you to retain your position in the schools of this city," she snapped.

During her San Diego sojourn, Helen made the acquaintance of the Cave Couts family and spent some three weeks at their elegant twenty-two-room hacienda in what is now Vista. The senior Couts had been a young lieutenant in the First Dragoons in 1849 when he met and married Ysidora Bandini, daughter of Don Juan Bandini and his wife, Dolores Estudillo. (Readers of *Two Years Before the Mast* are familiar with Don Juan.) The Couts's land was said to have been a wedding gift from the bride's sister, María Francisca Paula Arcadia Bandini Stearns. It was a lovely windfall for a young officer just starting out, but scarcely to be missed by the Stearnses, whose lands were among the most extensive in the state. Present-day Long Beach is but a small part of the Stearnses' Alamitos Ranch, which comprised thousands of acres extending from San Pedro to San Bernardino.

Helen, it turned out, was distantly related to the family forebear Don Abel Stearns, a soldier-of-fortune type who'd also married into the illustrious Estudillo clan, introducing a Yankee work ethic into the aristocratic strain. Had Don Abel Stearns still been alive, he and Helen might have amused themselves by tracing their heritage back to the same Salem Puritan, Isaac Stearns.

Instead, Helen heard another story. While staying at the Couts's hacienda, Helen met a young Indian woman named Ramona who told her of the murder of her husband, Juan Diego, by a brutal American settler, Sam Temple. Ramona's husband had suffered from a mental disorder causing occasional lapses of memory. During one of those lapses, Diego mistakenly substituted Temple's horse for his own, riding the other man's mount up the steep mountain trail to his cabin. When Temple emerged from the general store, he found Diego's stout Indian pony waiting patiently at the hitching rack. His own horse was an ancient rickety mare — not the splendid black he later described. Temple might have been better advised to let the trade stand at least temporarily, but became furious at the idea that an Indian would have made off with his property.

Temple loaded his double-barreled shotgun, draped a six shooter around his thick waist, and rode off in pursuit. When he reached the Diego home, it was Ramona who greeted him in the doorway, an ailing baby in her arms. At the sound of Temple's angry voice, Juan came out and walked toward his accusor who had dismounted. Still confused, Juan insisted the horse was his. "*Mío*," he repeated again and again as Temple raised his shotgun and leveled it at him.

Determinedly Temple fired; sixty-three shots were found in Diego's body. When the man still moved, Temple struck him with the empty shotgun, breaking the stock over the Indian's head. Ramona watched as the angry white man drew his pistol and fired three times point-blank into her husband's head. She cradled his body in her arms while Temple rode off, later to brag of not only having retrieved his "hoss" but of killing an Indian as well. The man had gone free; the event forgotten except by Temple, who still liked to boast about it, and the widow, Ramona.

The latter would recall an encounter that later seemed fated, a meeting with the "fine lady" guest at the Couts hacienda. "She spoke soft and sweet to me about how Juan got killed and I cry with her and tell her how I loved him. She wrote it all down on paper what I tell her," Ramona said later.

Helen's horror was renewed by this new tale of savagery. Was it true? she asked Señora Couts. Her hostess shrugged. The event had been common knowledge at the time, the details unimportant to her.

What had begun as a warm friendship with Doña Ysidora and her son, Cave, Jr., began to cool. Looking about at the impressive home that the late Major Couts had designed combining American frame architecture with Mexican tile and adobe, Helen could see nothing but the trappings of rank and privilege. The building was constructed around a tinkling fountain with fruit trees and climbing roses. Beyond this tranquil oasis were extensive corrals, barns, stables, and servants' quarters. Their land stretched farther than the eye could see, but apparently this wasn't enough. Helen had learned that the Couts family was even now litigating to remove the La Jolla Indians from their reservation. There had also been complaints from the Pala Indians, who claimed that Cave Couts had confiscated some of their sheep.

Helen was shocked by the stories and planned to investigate them. In the meantime it was impossible for her to remain silent when she observed how little the

Indian employees were fed and how much was expected of them. Both mother and son were furious at their guest's meddling and accused Helen of inciting the servants to rebel against their authority. Helen's stay at Rancho Guajome ended abruptly.

But as novelists are often able to do, she did manage to have the last word, and it has lasted for more than one hundred years. At the time of Helen's visit, Couts was a young man languishing on the verandah. He'd injured his leg and was being pampered back to health by his solicitous mother. Some of Couts's resentment of Helen, which he carried well into his eighties, probably came for his appearance in the pages of *Ramona* as the tender-hearted but incredibly ineffectual young lord of the manor, Felipe. If Couts was piqued, his mother, Doña Ysidora, must have been furious at the portrait of herself as the arrogant and conniving villainess in the piece.

Concurrent with Helen's field trips was the running battle over the rights of the Saboba Indians. Upon her initial return to California, she and Co had gone directly to Saboba where they had found the situation every bit as grim as Mary Sheriff had indicated in her letter. The Indians were threatened by eviction at any moment. When Helen attempted to pursue the matter with S. S. Lawson, the local Indian agent, she got nowhere. Lawson made it clear that he had no intention of locking horns with local dignitaries and resented her interference.

Now, the fact-finding mission complete, the party was back at the Kimball Mansion in Los Angeles. A very weary Newell Mitchell took his horses and wagon — much the worse for wear — and returned to his livery stable in Anaheim. Henry Sandham collected his drawings and took the train east. It was time for Helen to assemble her recommendations for the Bureau of Indian Affairs; in the meantime however, something had to be done for the Sabobas.

It seemed the only avenue remaining to them was one suggested by Co. Helen decided to pursue it. On May 20 she wrote to Mary Sheriff: "One more line just before setting off to say that I have at this last moment made a positive arrangement with the law firm, Brunson & Wells to defend the Saboba Indians *even it* the government does not authorize them to do it– –I could not bear to go away & leave the matter in such shape that there could be the *least* chance of their not getting a chance at whatever hope there may be for them in the law. — So I have myself guaranteed to the lawyers a certain sum for which they will undertake to *see the case through* if a suit of enactment is brought against the village.

"It is now done what human agency can do — and I must say I feel very confident that those Indians will not be moved. Mr. Wells is *greatly* interested in the case — is a very warm hearted humane man and he thinks they will win the case.

"You must write directly to him immediately if anything happens that you think he ought to know, but above all *make* the Captain understand the importance of his being on the *watch* — and if any papers of any kind are served on any of the Indians to bring them here immediately to Mr. Wells & tell *nobody*."

Helen believed that it was essential to the success of the plan that the Indians do nothing to arouse the suspicion of the white settlers in the area, that they appear resigned to their fate. She hoped in that way to stall for precious time. "The only loophole," she continued, "that I can see for an accident is in the Indians themselves being either careless — or suspicious about going to a lawyer — but you must labor with them, till you get it clear in their minds — & make them understand that they will not have to pay the lawyers anything. If the Government does not assume the case, *I will*! I can beg enough money to make up what I cannot pay myself. I know, & at any rate I have guaranteed it — & Mr. Wells has promised to do all that can be done. Yours ever, H J. I am off tonight."

On June 1 Will's newest enterprise, The Antlers Hotel, opened. The "noble structure," fronting on Pike's Peak Avenue, was reported to have cost one hundred thousand dollars. Helen may well have been the only one in town who didn't attend the gala opening. She was home alone working on her report.

Toward the end of the month, Co joined her. He went over the completed manuscript and offered only minor suggestions. "You're the writer, General," he reminded her, "I trust your judgment completely." Fifty-six pages long, the report later appeared as an appendix to *A Century of Dishonor*. It dealt primarily with the mission Indians in the three southernmost California counties and included some mention of the fugitive tribes on the outskirts of the Riverside County, San Bernardino, and the San Gabriel Valley — she described them as "gypsies in brush huts."

Following a short history of each band, Helen made her recommendations:

1. The Indians' reservations should be determined by resurveying, rounding out, and distinctly marking.

2. All white settlers now on reservations should be removed.

3. Indian villages now within confined grants the Government should either remove and make other provision for, or uphold and defend their right to remain. [In support of the second course, the written opinion of Brunson and Wells was appended.]

4. All Indian reservations should be patented to the several bands occupying them, the United States to hold the patent in trust for twenty-five years and then convey it to the Indians, as was done with the Omahas in Nebraska.

5. The number of schools should be increased, women teachers employed.

6. Indian agents and physicians should be required to visit each village twice a year.

7. The law firm of Brunson and Wells in Los Angeles should be appointed to act as special United States attorneys in all cases affecting the Indians.

8. Agricultural implements and farm equipment should be distributed among the Indians.

9. A small fund should be provided for the purchase of food and clothing for the very old and the sick in times of special destitution.

10. Should the Government decide to remove Indian villages on land already patented and to provide new quarters for their establishment, two purchases of land, one positively, the other contingently, were recommended.

11. Several small bands of Mission Indians north of the boundaries of the so-called Mission Indians' Agency should be included in the rehabilitation. These were specifically the San Carlos near the ranch, San Francisquita of Monterey, and those in the neighborhood of the Missions San Antonio de Padua, San Miguel, and Santa Inez.

Helen gave Commissioner Price a long list of influential persons, which included every member of Congress, and asked him to send them copies. Then, once again, she sat back and waited.

The response took a curious and disappointing form. Shortly after publication, Helen received a letter from Mary Sheriff. The schoolteacher's salary was being cut to a pittance. Both women believed it was an act of open retaliation. Determined that the Indian children not be deserted, Helen made up the difference herself.

Despondent, Helen cast about for something to do. The summer was dragging on and there had been no congressional response. Perhaps it was naive to imagine that she could influence the American people and their appointees with cold hard facts. Was it indeed necessary to persuade them with a novel — the kind of work J. B. Gilder had suggested two years earlier? Could she, Helen Hunt Jackson, move a nation and right a wrong with just a story?

Although she finally had the material for a novel, its form eluded her. For once Helen's mind was blank. Then, late in October, she awoke one morning with a start. "Before I was wide awake, the whole plot flashed into my mind," she later wrote Higginson. "In less than five minutes, as if someone spoke it, I sprang up, went to my husband's room and told him. I was half frightened."

CHAPTER TEN

The Sugar Pill

"It was sheep-shearing time in Southern California," Helen's pencil flew across her yellow notepad. She was only vaguely aware of the snow falling on Fifth Avenue.

Colorado Springs had proven just too "social" for her, with far too many distractions. Perhaps she regarded Will as one of them. At any rate she informed him that she would have to go to New York to write her projected California novel.

"But your niece is coming," he reminded her.

Helen's jaw dropped. In the excitement of her vision, she'd forgotten the request from her sister, Ann. It concerned her namesake, Helen Banfield, who'd graduated from Vassar three years earlier and who was now twenty-four, unmarried, and frail. Ann hoped that a winter in Colorado would improve her daughter's health, as it had her sister's years before. After Helen's return from California, they'd exchanged numerous letters full of plans for the visit. The young woman was soon to arrive, expecting to be taken about and introduced into local society. It would be impossible for Helen to manage that and do justice to her novel as well. Will would simply have to do it for her. After all, she reminded him, he'd have Effie, her maid-of-all-work. to run the house.

If Will thought New York City a strange place to write a narrative about California, he didn't comment. It was clear that he'd been only half aware of his wife's excited account of her visionary plot. He was absorbed in his own problems — work stoppage on the railroad line and stock manipulations by wily eastern financiers. Will had scarcely heard Helen, but now he nodded an equally absent-minded agreement to her insistence that he look after her visiting niece. Helen's mind had already slipped back to the story that demanded to be written. She reasoned vaguely that having a young woman about might be a pleasant change for Will. She could scarcely have guessed how pleasant.

Helen arrived in New York on November 20, 1883, and settled into her favorite hotel, The Berkeley, on the corner of Fifth Avenue and Ninth Street. If for whatever obscure reason she thought it better not to do her writing in California, she at least contrived to bring California with her to New York. In trunks and boxes all around the room were her "traps" — as Will called them — baskets, weavings, embroideries, in the rich warm colors of the golden state.

Once she'd arranged everything to her satisfaction, Helen began a flurry of appeals to her California friends for the details needed to bring her story to life. To the Coronels she confided: "I am going to write a novel, in which will be set forth some Indian experiences in a way to move people's hearts. People will read a novel when they will not read serious books. The scenes of the story will be in Southern California, and I shall introduce enough of Mexicans and Americans to give it variety. The thing I want most, in the way of help, from you in this: I would like an account written in as much detail as you remember of the time when you, dear Mr. Coronel, went to Temecula and marked off the boundaries of the Indians' land there. How many Indians were living there then? What crops had they? Had they a chapel? etc. . . . The Temecula ejection will be one of the episodes in my story and any and every detail in connection with it will be of value to me. . . . I wish I had had this plan in mind when I was in Los Angeles. I would have taken notes of many interesting things you told me. But it is only recently, since writing out for our report the full accounts of the different bands of Indians there, that I have felt that I dared undertake the writing of a long story."

Of her friend in San Diego, Ephraim Morse, Helen also inquired about the Temecula incident and asked about "the taking of a lot of sheep from some of the Pala or San Luis Rey Indians by Major Couts." She explained that she was planning to write a book, but urged him "not to speak of this." Helen hoped to keep her project a secret for the time being from all but close friends. Too much early talk might dull its impact.

Mary Sheriff was another source. To her, Helen directed an inquiry regarding Sam Temple, the man who'd gunned down the Indian Juan Diego. Helen wanted to know exactly how — if at all — justice worked in San Diego County. How did they impanel a jury, and how many jurors were there? Where did they meet? What did the judge say? What did Sam Temple say? Was he sworn in? Was he ever detained at all? "Any & every detail you can get will be of value," Helen urged at the last.

To a Mr. Eagan she explained, "I want very much to know what would be the Indian name for 'Blue Eyes' and for 'Wild Wood Dove.' Can you find out for me?" Whatever his answer, it didn't suit her. By return mail Helen wrote back: "The name for Blue Eyes will not do. I am sorry. Will you ask the old woman what it would be for 'Eyes of the Sky'? I dare say that would be no less dissonant and complicated, but I would be exceedingly glad if I could get an explicit word that would be melodious and pleasing for a child's name and yet *mean* blue eyes. The other name, the wood dove, if I read your word correctly, is mayel — is that it? To that I shall add the termina, making it majella, an exceedingly pretty name with a charming significance."

The time finally came when Helen could begin to actually write. On the desk before her — beside the portrait of her son Rennie, which accompanied Helen on all her travels — she placed a photograph of a young couple set against a halo of clouds. They were her inspiration, the hero and heroine she would bring to life: he, an Indian sheep shearer named Alessandro — after a bright young chief she'd met on her travels — the woman, the beautiful Ramona.

Helen wrote every day and usually long into the night, scribbling on at what she would later describe to Higginson as "lightning speed," turning out one and sometimes two thousand words in a single session. "I have never done half that amount of work in the same time," she marveled.

But the cost was dear. It was a dreadful winter; Helen, working as fast and frantically as she did, had rarely felt worse. Alternating between marathon writing stints and periods of total exhaustion, she scarcely knew whether to blame the frantic pace or the awful weather for her recurrent illnesses. She was certain only of the urgent need to continue, to complete her work. Compulsively, she plunged on, plagued always by a nagging sense that time was running out.

"As soon as I began, it was impossible to write fast enough," she admitted to Higginson. "It racks me like an outside power. I cannot help being superstitious about it. Twice, since beginning it, I have broken down utterly for a week. What I have to endure holding myself away from it, no words can tell. It is like keeping from a lover whose hand I can reach."

Helen had begun work December 1. A month later she wrote her friend William Hayes Ward at the *Independent*, confiding her dream: "If I can do one-hundredth part for the Indian what Mrs. Stowe did for the Negro, I will be thankful. . . . I would like to consult you about the title. 'In the Name of the Law' is so good a title that I feel as if it must have been used before but the literary friends I consulted say not. Have you ever heard a story by that title?"

In another letter she complained of the snow, so thick that she couldn't leave the hotel and had to send a boy out to obtain copies of the *Independent* at Brentano's so that she could read her mission Indian articles. Referring again to her new work, Helen confided her strategy. She hoped to sugar her pill, masking her message in the romantic aura of old California. In an effort to create atmosphere, Helen ignored the wind and snow outside and tried to evoke memories of brilliant sunshine and the sharp outlines of amber hills. A sense of warmth and color was essential, and Helen searched her memory for scenes to weave into her narrative.

She'd drawn vivid word pictures of two of her most important characters, the stern, implacable Señora Moreno and her effete son, Felipe. Next it was necessary to describe their home. Mother and son had been inspired by Doña Ysidora and Cave Couts; Helen, always mindful of libel, thought it wise to go no further. The all-important setting for the early part of her story would need to be some place other than Rancho Guajome. She would have to come up with a locale as elegant, yet with a few striking differences.

At last Helen thought of Rancho Camulos with its still-splendid hacienda surrounded by flowering orange groves, silver-leaved olive trees, and sunburnt hills. She'd stopped there for only two hours two years earlier while en route to Santa Barbara. The owner, Señora del Valle, had been away at the time of Helen's visit, and she had been able to see only the exterior of the house yet well remembered the picturesque setting.

Transcending time and space, Helen reached across the miles, calling from memory the clear, hot noondays and quickly falling nights, the golden fields of ripening grain, and the dull, autumn tints of the California landscape before the winter rains. It was essential to the success of her story to capture the mystique of bygone days, to beguile her readers with images of an idealized past reachable only through imagination.

Higginson had urged Helen — possibly fearing for her health — to calm down and write more slowly; but she interpreted his caution as concern for the quality of her work. "You will ask," she reassured him, "what sort of English I write at this lightning speed. So far as I can tell, the best I ever wrote!" But despite her passion, Helen remained a pragmatist. The bills had to be paid, and it was sometimes necessary to take time off from her novel to write poems and essays. These went out at regular intervals, often followed by bitter complaints after publication regarding errors in the text. (Probably the editors and printers were unable to interpret her deplorable handwriting.) Always, however, she returned to the all-consuming novel.

"The success of it," she explained to Higginson, "if it succeeds, will be that I do not even suggest any Indian history till the interest is so aroused in the heroine and hero, that people will not want to lay the book down.

"Every now and then I force myself to stop and write a story or a bit of verse; I can't bear the strain; but the instant I open the pages of the other, I write as I am writing now — as fast as I can copy! What do you think? Am I possessed of a demon? Fifty-four last October — and I'm not a bit steadier headed, you see, than ever! I don't know whether to send this or burn it up. Don't laugh at me whatever you do."

The whole story, she felt, was at her "finger ends," and Helen could have no peace until it was completed. On February 2 she wrote Co: "Whether from the horrible weather or from overwork I don't know, I collapsed for a week, and had an ugly sore throat and did no work. Now I am all right again and back at my table, but shall go slower. I am leading a life as quiet as if I were at Mrs. Kimball's — I go nowhere — am never out after 5 p.m. I am resolved to run no risks whatever till after I get this story done. Am pretty sure the 1st of March will see it done. Then I will play.

"The weather has been horrible — snow after snow; raw and cloudy days, — I have sighed for southern California. But in the house I have been comfortable — have not once seen the mercury below 60 in my rooms. The apartment is sunny and light — 6th floor — east windows — all my 'traps,' as Mr. Jackson calls them, came in well, and the room looks as if I had lived in it all my life."

As busy as she was, Helen still found time for her ongoing battles. "Miss Sheriff," she continued to Co, "writes me that a suit is brought for the ejectment of the Saboba Indians. Let me know if you have heard of it — what Brunson & Wells say. I wrote Wells asking for information about the suit by which the Temecula Indians were ejected — but he has not replied.

"What do you hear of the new agent? I got Miss Sheriff's salary restored to the old figure. . . . I wish they'd [the government] send us again somewhere. They never will. I've had my last trip as a 'Junketing Female Commissioner.'

"Do write soon; — and answer all my questions — and don't wait for me to reply, but write again. I am writing from 1,000 to 2,000 words a day on the story and letters are impossible, except to Mr. Jackson. Whether I write or not you know I am always the same affectionate old General. . . ."

On February 20 she wrote again: "There is a bill of some sort prepared and before Congress. I have written to Teller asking for it, or sum and substance. He does not reply. None of them care for anything now, except the election. . . .

"I am working away at the story — twenty chapters done. I'd like to consult you. Do you think it will do any harm to depart from the chronological sequence of events in my story? For dramatic purposes I have put the Temecula ejectment before the first troubles in San Pasquale. Will anybody be idiot enough to make a point of that? I am not writing history. I hope the story is good.

"I wish you could see my rooms. What with my Indian baskets, the things from Marsh's, and antique rugs, they are really charming, luckily for me who have been shut up in them by the solid week.

"Such weather was never seen. There are no words for it — proper ones — suitable to describe it. I sigh for San Gabriel sunshine.

"I hope you are well and jolly. I'm awfully sorry you are not married. Good night." She signed herself, "Always, affectionately yours, General."

By April she'd finished the twenty-sixth, and last, chapter. Helen Hunt Jackson had written 150,000 words in four months. Against the rich backdrop of Southern California, she'd constructed the poignant story of Ramona, the ward of an aristocratic Californio family, and her Indian lover, Alessandro.

The drama begins when Ramona is forced to flee from her cruel and despotic stepmother. She and Alessandro are married by a sympathetic frontier priest. Adapting quickly to Indian ways, Ramona is happy with Alessandro until the Anglos move in and take over the tribe's land. They make a new start in a remote valley near Saboba, but once again are driven out by white settlers. This time they take refuge on an isolated mountain where their baby dies from lack of medical attention. Alessandro suffers a nervous breakdown and, in a state of confusion, inadvertently substitutes a white settler's horse for his own. The angry American tracks Alessandro to his mountain cabin and kills him before Ramona's eyes.

Helen's "sugar pill" often appears saccharine by today's standards — though it remains in print and continues to sell briskly — yet behind the melodrama is a story as clear as a photograph. Shaded by the tints of an old romance is a factual account of the American doctrine of manifest destiny.

Helen completed her work at 11 P.M. on March 8, 1884. On May 1 the *Christian Union* announced that it would soon be serializing a new novel in weekly installments. That departure from its usual once-a-month format was Helen's idea. She wanted to get her message across in a hurry. On Monday 15 the first installment of the story that she had finally decided to call *Ramona* appeared beneath the byline Helen Hunt Jackson. The editors had added in parentheses H. H., to at last identify the author to her vast reading public.

Unfortunately, Helen was too ill to enjoy the fanfare. This time it was more than the recurring sore throat that had plagued her throughout the long, hard winter. She had collapsed, totally exhausted. Dr. C. L. Nichols, the homeopathic physician called in to attend her, shared none of Dr. Cate's enthusiasm for Colorado. His prescription was that Helen stay away from there for two years and refrain from all "brain work."

Tired as she was, Helen had to laugh. She missed Will, and brain work was her life. "I'd rather die," she declared emphatically. When Nichols warned her that a nervous breakdown could be worse than death, she ignored him. If nothing else, their disagreement gave her the shot of adrenalin necessary to get up and pack her bags.

On June 2 she stopped at the *Independent* with a poem and a note that she asked the office boy to deliver to William Hayes Ward, who was closeted in his inner office. She requested immediate payment for the poem and for some others she'd sent him the Saturday before, explaining that she was leaving that very day for Colorado Springs and was short of cash. Helen asked for from sixty-five to seventy-five dollars and offered to "square" the bill with another poem to be mailed later if he thought it necessary. "I do think Mr. Bowen ought not to mind paying on acceptance once a year," she argued, adding "the *Independent* is the only paper that does not pay me on acceptance for everything." She got her seventy-five dollars.

Back at last in Colorado Springs after an absence of more than six months, she was surprised to hear that her niece, Helen — now departed — had stayed nearly that long. Will had been a most conscientious host, taking her on picnics and horseback rides into the mountains. Effie, the maid, saw to it that Helen heard all about how her niece had assumed the role of mistress of the house and had served as Will's hostess. During that same period, the Denver and Rio Grande Railroad had filed for bankruptcy, and Will had been appointed receiver. His responsibilities for reorganizing the company apparently hadn't interfered with his social life.

What Helen may have thought about all of this went unrecorded, but she was not about to go to bed as the doctor had ordered. Once again, she busied herself redecorating the house. A small lift was installed to carry coal and other heavy burdens to the second floor. Crates containing more "traps" had arrived from her friends in California. Helen delighted in arranging animal skins and Indian artifacts, a rug handmade for her by an old Saboba woman, embroidered sheets from the bed of the Indian captain, Jesús.

With the publication of *Ramona*, Helen felt that a great burden had been lifted. She believed that she had done her best, given the fullest measure of her talent and energy. Now she could begin to relax and enjoy life as she never had before.

In a quick note to Co, she spoke of her sense of well-being; never had she had "such a sense of delight in the prospect of the summer."

CHAPTER ELEVEN

Another Kind of Battle

On Saturday, June 28, 1884, Helen — hurrying as usual — caught the heel of her slipper and fell headlong the entire length of her stairway.

"I could recall nothing after the first tripping of my foot and a vain clutch at the balistrade," she later wrote Co. "If we had a free hand rail as we ought I should not have fallen."

It was a wonder, Helen marveled later, that she hadn't broken her neck. As it was, the fall resulted in a compound fracture that would cripple her for life. Her left leg smashed, Helen was unable to move for weeks.

Effie, the housemaid, proved a cheerful and efficient nurse. Helen had need of solace from someone. Will was "never home except for a Sunday or overnight, but in Denver most of the time." For once, Helen was glad of his absence. "I dread having people know I am an invalid," she admitted to Effie, "and most of all Mr. Jackson."

Helen had her bed brought down to the dining room, where she could feel more a part of things while enjoying an unobstructed view of her beloved Cheyenne Mountain. Her leg encased in a plaster cast, she was grateful for the pleasant weather which was "mercifully cool and moist" that summer.

For a time she indulged herself reading "silly novels," but other people's writing soon palled. Before long she was at work on another "sugar pill" — this one for children. It pleased her to construct a novel set in a spot very like Co's Kinneyloa. In *The Hunter Cats of Connor-loa* she managed to capture the whole menage — bachelor master, mulatto majordomo, twenty Chinese coolies, seventeen cats, a bevy of rabbits, moles, linnets, snakes, and even a tame baby skunk. To them, Helen added two children, Susy and Rea, who came to the rescue of an Indian about to be evicted from his land by an Anglo settler.

"You will laugh to see yourself saddled with an orphan niece and nephew," she told Co. "I hope you won't dislike the story. I propose in the next to make you travel all through Southern California with 'Susy and Rea'—and tell the Indian story over again." Once more Helen was taking potshots at real people. "I only hope that scalawag C——, of Los Angeles, will come across the story, and see himself set forth in it. He will recognize the story of Fernando, the old Indian he turned out of San Gabriel."

By August Helen was allowed to get out of bed twice a day to sit in a wheelchair; then finally the cast was removed, and she could take her first step on crutches. It was a proud moment; she thought it "a remarkable success for an old woman past fifty" who'd gained too much weight from inactivity.

The privacy that Helen had hoped for was not to be hers. Without realizing it and against her will, she had become a celebrity. Everything that she did was considered news. It wasn't long before an account of the accident appeared in newspapers throughout the country. One of the first friends to respond was Emily Dickinson. Her concern was deep and genuine.

Helen's reply was chatty and cheerful despite her restrictions. After answering Emily's questions about the fall and wryly discussing life in a wheelchair, she moved on to a familiar topic: "What portfolios of verses you must have. — It is cruel wrong to your 'day & generation' that you will not give them light. — If such a thing should happen as that I should outlive you, I wish you would make me your literary legatee & executor. Surely, after you are what people called 'dead' you will be willing that the poor ghosts you have left behind, should be cheered and pleased by your verses, will you not? — You ought to be. — I do not think we have a right to with hold from the world a word or thought any more than a *deed*, which might help a single soul."

As always, Emily's reply was prompt, but still a holdout. The issues of publication and executorship were pointedly ignored. She was happy that her friend had "taken Captivity Captive" and rejoiced "that that martial Verse has been verified. 'He who is slain and smiles, steals something from the Sword,' but you have stolen the Sword itself, which is far better — I hope you may be harmed no more — I shall watch your passage from Crutch to Cane with jealous affection. From there to your Wings is but a stride —— "

The recent weeks had been bad for Emily as well. "I, too," she wrote, "took my summer in a Chair, though from 'nervous prostration,' not fracture, but take my Nerve by the Bridle now, and am again abroad. Thank you for the wish —— " She signed herself "Loyally, E. Dickinson."

Helen's doctor had assured her that she would soon be walking on a cane and that her leg would eventually be as good as ever, but she remained doubtful. "I shall believe it when I see it!" she admitted to Co.

The idea of being "cooped up in Colorado" for the winter depressed her. As always, Helen was certain that a change of environment would make her better. Two or three months of "sunshine and outdoors in Southern California" would soon have her well again. She'd been disappointed to learn that Mrs. Whipple had closed her boardinghouse in San Diego — a climate she herself preferred — and moved to Los Angeles. Now Helen asked Co about the new location, "Is it on *high* ground?"

Her letter crisscrossed with Kinney's, which contained an exciting surprise. He'd fallen in love at last and wanted to bring his bride to Colorado Springs for their honeymoon.

When he described his fiancée as a "young H. H.," Kinney was saying a lot. He'd been immediately drawn to Helen and — many years later — would vividly recall their initial meeting, "Her brightness, vivacity and keen interest in everything she saw attracted me to her, as it did everybody else." It was high praise for a man young enough to be her son, and months of close association did nothing to diminish his admiration. He described Helen as "a wonderful traveling companion, her sympathies and knowledge were so broad. Everything appealed to her — the flowers, trees, insects, the ocean, the clouds, the stars, the different colored rocks, the farms and their crops, and especially the people. Nothing escaped her, and when it came to human beings she seemed to have intuitions that were more than human. She could go up to utter strangers, people of the most diverse kinds, — and in a few minutes, without any leading or prompting, they seemed to pour out their inmost ideas to her."

Helen was delighted by the news, she'd been urging her Co to find a wife. Naturally she was full of questions and certainly must have felt a little uneasy at the possibility of losing her favorite completely. Her response was dated October 5, 1884:

> There are but two things in life which could have pleased me more than the news in the last letter of yours. Really in love, you are, are you? "Way in deep" — the only way there's any use of being. I always hoped you had it in you, but your cold-blooded way of talking about "*a* wife," made me a little afraid.
>
> Now are you glad you didn't marry that horrid W —girl! I want to know all about Miss Margaret Thompson—
> Dark or light
> Short or tall
> Stout (!) or slender
> Pretty? — (of course).

Vivacious or quiet?

Gentle or will-full?

I hope the latter. I hope she'll make you mind! But oh dear, oh dear, why do you come to Colorado when I am away — above all things when I am in Southern California! You know I always have to *fly* in October for fear of our snows which set in then, and invariably give me bronchitis. . . .

I am endlessly chargrined that you must needs have fixed your wedding trip to Colorado at a time when I can't have you in my house. How I should have enjoyed putting you in my blue room! And Mr. Jackson even is never here now. He is in Denver all the time! It is too, too bad. Just put off being married, will you, till next June, and come and spend a month with me then! I am vain enough to think (which vexes me still more) that it must have been chiefly to see me and show HER to me that you were going to take your journey in this direction. You surely would not think of taking a journey to Colorado for pleasure in November! . . .

I wish you would give my love — if I may — to your Margaret. Tell her I implore her to like me! I am afraid she won't. That's the worst of loving either men or women before they are married! God bless you, dear fellow, and give you all the happiness possible on this earth.

Ever affty yours,

H. J.

P.S. You will wonder what the two things are which would have pleased me more yesterday than your letter. First, to have a whole leg in place of this broken one. Second, to have Mr. Jackson tell me that he would give up Colorado and go to live at some *Christian* altitude, and before settling down, travel for a few years. — I'll never have either of these two things, so I'm glad you have your wife.

At Helen's request Mrs. Whipple had sent her the floor plan of the new boardinghouse at 439 Pearl Street (originally Grasshopper and later Figueroa). By October 12 Helen made her selection — two first-floor rooms at the back. "I would be glad of that little side entrance, while I am so helpless," she explained in her letter, "one hates to be a spectacle."

One month later, accompanied by Effie, Helen departed once more for California. She had no qualms about starting out a cripple on such a far journey. As always, looking ahead to new possibilities, she felt a fresh wave of optimism. Helen left 228 East Kiowa Street as she had always left it — without a backward glance.

Helen was soon "prancing about on the verandah" of Mrs. Whipple's boardinghouse — actually it was only a few minutes on her cane, but for a time even that seemed an improvement. At first she liked the large white house on a hill and found the other residents more stimulating than those she'd met at Mrs. Whipple's San Diego establishment. Then the rains came, early that year and unusually heavy. There was a cold chill about her rooms — the very thing she'd feared.

Co invited Helen to come to Kinneyloa, but she refused, explaining, "I am too helpless and troublesome to be comfortable anywhere except in a boarding-place." She hoped to be at her best when she finally met "young H. H."

Helen compromised with the Coronels, who wanted her to stay with them at El Recreo. She made long, almost daily visits, but spent nights at the boardinghouse. Once again the hospitality was lavish. Don Antonio sang for her and told his old-California stories. One can imagine what his companionship must have meant to Helen by her description of him in the article "Echoes in the City of the Angels": "He is sixty-five years of age, but he is young; the best waltzer in Los Angeles today; his eye keen, his blood fiery quick; his memory like a burning glass bringing into sharp focus a half century as if it were yesterday." Doña Mariana, too, was warm and vital, with the clear olive skin, soft brown eyes, and gentle smiling mouth of a Spanish madonna — a mature Ramona born into happier circumstances.

They were the best kind of friends, understanding and accepting as well as affectionate. Recognizing that what Helen needed most during her long and difficult convalescence was the sense of continuity and independence that only writing could give her, they provided not only comfort and solace but time and space as well.

Since Helen could write only in a reclining position, Don Antonio designed a special table for her — small and light, with two lower shelves for notes. Using this and lying on a couch, Helen wrote a number of poems and at least one article, "From Icicles to Oranges," — another paean to Southern California.

Whenever Helen had a manuscript ready to mail east, she and Doña Mariana made an outing of driving to the post office. One afternoon late in November they found a package there addressed to Helen. When she read Roberts Brothers above the return address, the author guessed the contents immediately: an advance copy of *Ramona*. After serialization in the *Christian Union,* the manuscript had been rushed into print with Christmas sales in mind. Helen had seen it listed in the November 8 issue of *Publishers Weekly,* but this was her first glimpse of the book itself.

She eagerly tore open the package. The cover was a pleasant surprise, golden artichokes against a green background. The same "great soft-round disks of fine straight threads like silk with a kind of saint's halo around them of sharp, stiff points" that she'd described in *Ramona.*

And there was her signature, Helen Jackson — a little neater than if she'd written it herself — with the familiar H. H. beneath it. Impulsively Helen reached into her reticule. Pulling out a pencil, she wrote quickly "With the compliments of the author" and handed the first copy of *Ramona* to her friend Mariana.

Then the anxious wait for the reviews. Friends had assured Helen again and again that *Ramona* was the best thing she'd ever written, but she herself was often doubtful. "I can't believe it is as good as they think," she admitted. "I am uneasy about it."

The initial reaction justified her concern. Helen had dreamed of writing another *Uncle Tom's Cabin,* but her task was far greater than Harriet Beecher Stowe's had been thirty years earlier. At that time slavery had been a burning issue, the public ready, eager, for a rallying point. In 1884 a social-protest novel championing the cause of the American Indian was both unlooked for and unwanted. The native American was viewed with indifference, if not hostility: "the only good Indian is a dead Indian." As a result, critics reviewed the romance and ignored the Indians. *Ramona* was described as "a sweet and mournful poetic story" and as "a prose Evangeline." It was faint praise for one whose whole purpose had been to incite righteous indignation. Worse yet, when angry protests did occur, they generally came from San Diego and were leveled at *her.* It was the settlers, not the Indians, who were championed by a vehement segment of society that bitterly resented her portrayal of Alessandro as saintly. It was a dark night of the soul for Helen, who couldn't know that *Ramona* would eventually become a classic, with a part yet to play in social history.

The rain continued steadily, and with it the chill dampness that contributed to Helen's discomfort. Add to that the angry words from Will, who'd written of his annoyance at an article that had recently appeared in the *Journalist* under the title "A Famous Literary Woman." Helen had been terribly indiscreet, he thought in talking so freely to a reporter; not only had she spoken candidly of her opinions on other writers, she had discussed *him.* Poor Helen — if there was anyone who guarded her privacy, it was she. The writer, Helen Bartlett, had gained her confidence by pretending to be an unpublished aspirant seeking advice. Nothing could have suited her purpose better. As always, generous with earnest newcomers to the profession, Helen had devoted many hours to Bartlett the previous summer, sharing not only the benefit of her own years of experience, but also honest evaluation of the work of others. Now it turned out that Helen Bartlett had actually been a correspondent on assignment from the *Milwaukee Sentinel* and had taken advantage of the opportunity to also write one in-depth profile for the *Journalist*. Helen was terribly hurt by Will's criticism. He should have *known* better. She was also furious at Bartlett's perfidy and wrote an angry letter to the *Sentinel* denouncing them for their employee's "bad faith."

As if that wasn't enough, Effie slipped and injured her knee. When the doctor came to examine her, he also took a look at Helen's good leg, which had lately been troubling her. She recounted the unhappy outcome in a letter to Co: "He says I must leave off trying to walk! Save it all I can. There is an inflammatory condition there, from the long overstrain of doing double duty and I must make up my mind to be on crutches for months! Cheerful —— all my prancing on the verandah and trying to do *all* I can have been a mistake. I must do as *little* as I can manage to get about with! The broken leg is gaining and except for my *whole* leg I could walk with a cane now! . . . ."

Helen tried to rally her spirits by going buggy riding with Effie. Sometimes they went all the way to Santa Monica "on roads where larks sing and flowers are in bloom" — or so she described them to Emily Dickinson. On the days when the rain kept her in bed, Helen tried to imagine herself looking across the sea to Japan.

Emily loved the fantasy. "That you compass Japan before you breakfast, not in the least surprises me, clogged only with Music, like the wheels of Birds," she replied. Emily reproached her own foot for being whole on behalf of Helen's lame one, gave high praises to *Ramona*, and closed, "Knew I how to pray, to intercede for your foot were intuitive, but I am but a Pagan."

It was now more than Helen's "foot" that troubled her. She was seriously ill. She had a persistent fever and nausea so violent that she was unable to eat. The weight that Helen would have loved to have lost earlier "poured" off — forty pounds in a little over a month — leaving her wan, yellow, and badly frightened.

Hoping a sea change would help, she moved briefly to Long Beach, but returned sicker than before. She would make no complaint to Will. Perhaps she was hurt by his reaction to the *Journalist* article, or possibly she thought him too busy with his own concerns to be troubled by hers. As a receiver for the railroad, Will was responsible for the failing fortunes of hundreds of investors. Instead, Helen turned to Co. "Nothing ever before so upset me," she wrote him.

Once again a new locale promised the answer. Someone had heard of a marvelous homeopathic physician in San Francisco. He would cure her, Helen felt certain, and she decided to take the train north. Once away from the chill of Mrs. Whipple's boardinghouse, she would be well again.

"I am very, very ill — go to San Francisco tomorrow," Helen informed Co on March 12, 1885. "Must have better medical care and more comfort.

"Miss Thibault has found a place for me, — corner of Sutter and Leavenworth Sts. Hope it is not full of sewer gas! . . . If I get desperately ill in S.F., I will telegraph for you to come up and look after me. Will you?" She signed the note "Your aff. General."

Leave-takings were cruel. The Coronels came with her to the railroad station. Miller, Helen's former driver, helped carry her belongings on board, then stood before her, speechless, his eyes filling with tears. Don Antonio put his arms around her. Unable to control his emotion, he sobbed, "Excuse me, I must!" Only Helen refused to cry. She knew that none of them expected to see her again alive. She forced a smile; it was up to her to cheer them up. She must put forth her last shred of energy to prove them wrong.

The whistle hooted, and Helen waved to them from the window. This time the smile was real. Once more she was on her way.

Helen's new San Francisco doctor had advised her to abandon all reading and writing if she was to prolong her life, but it was an impossible dictum. She would temporarily forsake reading, but *writing* never. "I must write," she told him. "I can't just lie here and have my friends and Mr. Jackson think I have forgotten them."

To Co, she commiserated: "Sorry you have to change cooks. Changing stomachs is worse however. Don't grumble, lest a worse thing befall you." She told him about her own diet — heated milk and gruel — then returned to an old theme in the postscript: "Can't you do something to get Rust appointed Indian agent? I have heard quite directly that Lamar is full of *warm* sympathy for the Indians. Do try, Co, and accomplish something for them. You might, if you determine to."

The end of June marked the anniversary of Helen's accident. It had been an "unlucky year" for her, and she saw little immediate hope of improvement. Still, her letter to the Coronels was full of lively enthusiasm. She'd interviewed Professor Charles Painter, a new appointee to the Indian Rights Association and was encouraged and impressed by his interest. An eastern magazine had asked her for a children's poem relating to a California incident or legend; she hoped Don Antonio would have a suggestion. She reminded them of some baskets she'd ordered from an Indian woman. Helen sent them money for the baskets — she feared the woman would think her "a lying white" if they weren't picked up soon — and asked to have them express mailed to her. "I have no doubt that I shall have to lie here for many weeks yet, and I shall enjoy having them," she explained. "Send with them also the flat one I gave you to keep. I'd like to keep work in it on my bed."

There was no doubt that Helen was digging in for a long siege. If she must at last accept the limitations of her condition, she wanted a room with a view. Obliging friends found just the place for her — a spacious apartment on Russian Hill at 1600 Taylor Street.

For once there was no joy in change; it was merely to be endured as a necessary evil. Grimly Helen suffered the carriage ride and hobbled into the building, assisted by Effie and the owner, Mrs. Helena Cheevers; but at the sight of the interior, her mood changed instantly. "I did not imagine that it would be so pleasant!" she exclaimed, happily surveying the soft gleam of the rosewood furniture, the light olive drapes turned to dull gold in the late afternoon sun. Most important was the view—tall windows opened out onto a small balcony—and from her bed Helen would be able to see both the Bay and Telegraph Hill.

With her usual candor and a total absence of self-pity, she added "What a beautiful place to die in."

CHAPTER TWELVE

Helen's Last Hurrah

Helen didn't like San Francisco; she never had.

On her arrival she'd confided to Co: "If I'd been asked to choose the one city of all I know in which I would have most desired not to be slain it would be San Francisco." But the commanding view beyond the rocky rise of Goat Island to the Oakland shore and beyond it to the purple outline of the Contra Costa hills was exhilarating. It stirred Helen to fresh possibilities.

She remembered the rugged grandeur of Yosemite and the Sierras. She thought of the clear, clean, pine-scented air and imagined herself sleeping out under the stars. Why couldn't she return to those mountains? Wouldn't it be possible to travel on a bed in the back of a wagon? The more Helen considered it, the stronger her resolve became.

"Let me try it," she urged her doctor. The young physician, usually so confident and full of optimism, looked dubious. Helen persisted, reasoning: "If the experiment doesn't kill me, I believe it will cure me. I shall go as a gamester throws in his last card." He agreed because he had to; Helen was determined to go anyway.

The trip had to be perfect. She wanted expert advice, and who could give it better than John Muir himself? Helen was an ardent admirer of the naturalist-explorer, whom she knew to be a former protégé of her friend Jeanne Carr. Jeanne had spoken often of the friendship that had developed when Muir was a student of her husband's years before at Wisconsin University. The two still corresponded; and although he was a few years older than Jeanne, Muir addressed her as "Dear, Dear Spiritual Mother."

Helen wrote immediately to Jeanne, asking for a letter of introduction. Then, unwilling to wait for formalities, communicated with him on her own. After introducing herself as a mutual friend of the couple who'd sponsored him during his undergraduate days, Helen spoke admiringly of Muir's work. She'd read every word of his that had ever been published — or at least told him so. "I never wished myself a man but once," she said, "and that was when I read how it seemed to be rocked in the top of a pine tree in a gale." Undoubtedly he recognized her reference to his "A Wind Storm in the Forest of Yuba."

Matter-of-factly Helen explained her situation. she retained only a teaspoon of food at a time — usually frozen custard. Often she felt so hot that she longed for the sound of rain and dreamed of lying for days in the fine spray of a waterfall. "I know with the certainty of instinct that nothing except three months out of doors day and night will get this poison out of my veins," she explained.

Helen then proceeded to list her requirements for the expedition: eight horses, a wagon for herself, a phaeton for Effie and the doctor, two camp wagons for tents and supplies, and four servants.

Startled, Muir asked, "What will my poor Douglass squirrels say at the sight?" Despite his reservations, he responded warmly, outlining several possible routes. Finally there was his prayer that God's sky would bend down to her as if made for Helen alone, and the pines spread their healing arms about her, to bless and make her well again.

Helen was so moved by his words that she insisted upon getting out of bed and sitting in her wheelchair. It was necessary, she explained to Effie, in order to build her strength for the marvelous adventure ahead. But even that small exertion proved too much. A total collapse followed, and Helen was forced to return to bed. This time there was no reprieve — not even in her dreams. She began to set her affairs in order.

Learning that Helen was in San Francisco, Flora Haines Apponyi came to call. The two had met years before in Colorado Springs prior to Helen's marriage. Their paths had separated only to converge again in Los Angeles, where Helen had gone to research her *Century* series on the Mission Indians. On that occasion Flora had found her friend much changed. The gaiety she'd remembered from Colorado Springs had dissipated, Helen seemed all "high purpose and commanding decision." Now, however, on entering the bedroom where Helen reclined propped up by pillows, she found to her surprise that "the gentle blue-eyed woman with her merry laugh" was back. She seemed not only at peace but happy.

The cancer that was destroying her wasn't discussed. Flora wrote later of "a gradual prostration of all the vital energies, under the influence of a powerful and irresistible disease." Her praise of Helen's limitless patience and courage was unstinting. The dying woman refused to even speak of her symptoms, "completely ignoring her weak bodily condition and entering into conversation with such spirit and zest that one forgot she was an invalid, and was conscious only of the clear analytical mind with its flashes of humor and of the great generous heart."

Helen's greatest concern was with Will, and at last she felt free to say everything that was in her heart. "I am sure I am not going to get well & I want to bid you goodbye while my mind is clear," she explained to him in a letter.

The possibility that her all-consuming efforts might yet benefit the Indians was her only consolation as she looked back over the last ten years of their marriage. "I realize how I have failed to be to you what I longed and hoped to be," she admitted, but urged, "it is not too late, my beloved, for you to have a wife and children and live the life that will satisfy your longings.

"It is the greatest hope of my heart that you will desire to marry our Helen. She will make you a pure, devoted, loving wife & a splendid mother for your children & will match your wishes and views far better than I have done. I have left her the bulk of my property, feeling that it would be wrong for me to let my grandfather's money go away from his heirs and that you do not need it. I hope you will think this was right. If you marry Helen, it will be a happiness to me in whatever world I am in to see her & her children heirs to all I had.

If you don't feel drawn to her — let me implore you, darling, to marry someone else *very soon* — do not live the life of a homeless, tie-less man any longer than you must — but be *sure* this time, dearest, to marry some one whose standards in all matters of living are like your own. Don't make the same mistake, love, — you will wonder I can write so calmly as this. I am writing as if I spoke to you from another world.

"Will, you have never known how deep my realization has been of the fact that I was not the *right* wife for you — regardless, I have loved you. With a different woman & with children at your knees, you could have been a different man — & a happier one. — God will give it to you yet — & it was time! — I am glad to go for your sake, my loved one. Forgive every pain and vexation I have ever given you & only remember that I loved you as few men are ever loved in this world. *Nobody* will ever love you so well — and that you will feel as the years go on — & I shall perhaps hear you say it to yourself one day as I am watching you. . . ."

Sometimes it pleased Helen to "fancy" herself "a ghost," but the practical side remained. The majority of her estate would go, as she'd told Will, to her niece, Helen Banfield, but there were also bequests to Will's two sisters; and Dr. Cate, who'd once "saved" her life by ordering her to Colorado, would receive one thousand dollars. She thought much about her friends and was anxious to settle accounts. Publishers with bills were instructed to make payments to various persons. Boxes of books and other personal possessions were sent to friends and relatives, among them Jenny Abbott Johnson — Helen's friend from the days of the Abbott Institute thirty years earlier — and Mary Sheriff. There was also an itemized list of the Colorado Springs possessions for Effie to dispose of later.

When these tasks were completed, Helen felt a warm sense of accomplishment. In a last letter to her closest woman friend and the companion of her first California adventure, Sarah Woolsey, she confided, "You can't think how strange it seems to be lying here and planning everything out that I can possibly arrange for everybody."

Finally the time had come when Will had to be summoned — something she'd resisted until the last. He arrived on August 2.

If Helen had any professional regrets it was that she had found her mission so late. It seemed to her now that only *A Century of Dishonor* and *Ramona* were of any consequence. The public had been indifferent to the former, the critics to the latter. Now, ironically enough, she learned from Roberts Brothers that *Ramona* gave every indication of being a runaway best seller. Despite the lackluster reviews, the public liked her sugar pill. It remained to be seen how the medicine would go down.

There was one last note to Mary Sheriff: "I am profoundly touched by the message of the captain. To think that the poor souls still believe in me when nothing has been done for them! Give him my grateful remembrance and tell him if you can about *Ramona*. Tell him that over a hundred thousand people have read that story and are sorry for the Indians that many good people are working to try to get justice done them by the Government that I believe the new secretary is their friend & the new president too & hope has not died in my heart, though the time is very long and bad men are in greater numbers than good men in the Great Council in Washington."

Still, Helen wasn't about to leave this world without a last appeal to Washington. Just four days before her death, she wrote to President Grover Cleveland: "From my death-bed I send you a message of heart-felt thanks for what you have already done for the Indians. I ask you to read my *Century of Dishonor*. I am dying happier for the belief I have that it is your hand that is destined to strike the first steady blow toward lifting this burden of infamy from our country, and righting the wrongs of the Indian race."

Thomas Niles, her editor at Roberts Brothers, had written her of his pleasure in his new office and his regret that she couldn't see it. Helen gathered up the nearly completed manuscript of her last novel, *Zeph*, and sent it off to him with final instructions.

She had no fear of death, she assured him. "It is only passing from one country to another. My only regret is that I have not accomplished more work; especially that it was so late in the day when I began to work in real earnest. But I do not doubt that we shall keep on working.

"There isn't so much difference, I fancy, between this life and the next as we think, nor so much barrier. I shall look in upon you in the new rooms some day; but you will not see me. Good-bye."

On the evening of August 8, Helen placed her hand in Will's, passing into a painless sleep from which she never awakened. Four days later, on August 12, 1885, she died.

CHAPTER THIRTEEN

The Final Journey

At the very hour of Helen's death, she had a visitor. It was John Muir. If she could not go to the mountains, he hoped to bring some sense of the mountains to her. No one answered his knock, and the shades were drawn. "Mrs. Jackson may have gone somewhere," he told his wife, and the two turned away.

A few days later, back again in Colorado Springs, Will received a note from Emily Dickinson: "Helen of Troy will die, Helen of Colorado, never. 'Dear friend, can you walk?' were the last words I wrote her — 'Dear friend, I can fly.' — her immortal reply."

Emily, who'd been born two months after Helen, would survive her lifelong friend by only nine months, dying on May 15, 1886.

Will did marry Helen Banfield, and the union was apparently a very happy one until the couple's seventh child died in infancy early in 1899. The loss had a devastating effect upon Mrs. Jackson, who lapsed into a severe depression. Finally a physician, believing that a change of scene might be beneficial, advised her to return east for an extended stay. During that interval the *San Diego Union* reported: "Mr. Will Jackson, a recent guest at the Hotel del Coronado, quietly visited many of the scenes made famous by *Ramona*. One can readily understand with what thought and reflections he would visit the scenes that became a part of his wife's very being." The Jacksons were reunited later that year in Colorado Springs, but the second Mrs. Jackson's melancholia increased until, in October of that year, her life was tragically ended with a self-inflicted gunshot wound. Will survived her by twenty years, living on in the old house until his death at eighty-three on June 3, 1919.

Thomas Wentworth Higginson also lived well into the twentieth century. It was difficult for young writers and activists to comprehend that Higginson, having long outlived his causes, had been the intimate of Emerson, let alone John Brown. Nevertheless, he continued to fill the Grand Old Man niche, writing and lecturing practically to his dying day. A last article appeared in the May 20, 1911, issue of *Outlook* — just eleven days after his death at eighty-eight. Higginson's pallbearers were young black soldiers who'd not yet been born when he took command of his regiment in 1862.

Abbot Kinney continued for a time to work on behalf of the Indians, but without Helen to encourage him, his interests soon returned to the elaborate real estate schemes that had made him wealthy. In 1885 he founded the seaside town of Ocean Park, and it was his Santa Monica Improvement Association that received the paving and landscaping contract for the road that would become Wilshire Boulevard, one of Los Angeles's most important arteries.

Toward the end of the century, Kinney announced that he was going to recreate Italy's ancient city of canals on a site that was nothing more than sand and swamp. He envisioned a cultural citadel, but the reality was something quite different. Kinney died of the same cancer that had taken his "General" so many years before, on November 14, 1920 — just two weeks short of his seventieth birthday. Almost immediately the canals were filled in, but the aura of fantasy and flair for the bizarre continues to make Venice, California, unique among resorts.

On her deathbed Helen had said: "I didn't write *Ramona;* it was written through me. My lifeblood went into all I had thought, felt and suffered for five years on the Indian question." Never in her wildest dreams could she have imagined the furor and controversy that her novel would create or the tide of tourism that it would unleash. Within thirty years authorities would consider fifty million dollars a conservative estimate of the revenue brought to Southern California as a result of *Ramona.*

Now that romantic old California no longer existed, easterners longed to savor it, and residents were only too happy to cater to the fantasy. Seventy-two Catholic churches claimed to be the authentic marriage place of Ramona and Alessandro. Every town where the train stopped, plus a few flag stations, touted itself as the heroine's true birthplace. Enterprising Indian women amassed small fortunes selling baskets and posing for pictures — each and every one the "real" Ramona.

Sam Temple, who'd inadvertently inspired the novel by killing the unfortunate Indian known locally as "Crazy Juan," achieved some renown by touting himself as "the man who shot Alessandro." Far from being ashamed of his act, he boasted of it and even attempted to find donors to bankroll his appearances at the world fairs in St. Louis and Chicago. Some disapproved, but Temple had sympathizers as well. As late as 1900 a writer on the *San Diego Union* described him as "a good fellow in his way." The killing of an Indian for alleged horse stealing was still considered by some to be justifiable homicide. "Once an Indian always an Indian" was a not uncommon sentiment. Temple died peacefully in his sleep in 1909.

Ramona continued in popularity, edition following edition. Thirty years after its original publication, the book continued to be hailed as the great American novel. Three movies, starring Lillian Gish, Dolores del Rio, and Loretta Young, succcessively, in the title role, were made. In 1923 the town of Hemet began its yearly Ramona Pageant. The second actor to portray Alessandro was a young man named Victor Jory. It was his first paying job as an actor, and he would return for ten years to appear in the role and later to direct the pageant, now fitting the event in between Broadway and movie roles. The Hemet production has given a start to many talented performers, among them Raquel Welch.

Helen Hunt Jackson would have been amazed by all the fuss, and possibly amused at the form some of it took, but she would certainly have been deeply disappointed that her sugar pill had so little effect upon her beloved Indians. She died believing that change was in the air, and for a time it was. Largely as a result of her efforts, an Indian Rights Association had formed in every major city. At one time there were twenty-two Indians' advocacy groups in Southern California; as of this writing there are four.

Twelve tribes remain in Ramona country — San Diego and Riverside counties — with twenty-one thousand Indians living on eleven thousand square miles of reservations. They are still controlled by the Federal Bureau of Indian Affairs. In 1986 grants for Indian aid were cut once more.

Ramona deserves much of the credit for passage of the Dawes Act in 1887. As a result, sixty acres of land were allotted to each head of an Indian household. Some eventually were forced to sell. Others have handed the land down from generation to generation. Many Indians remain as they did in Helen's time, living with the elements, changing as gradually as nature.

Bibliography

Allen, Margaret. *Ramona's Homeland*. Chula Vista: Denrich Press, 1914.

Bianchi, Martha Gilbert. *The Life and Letters of Emily Dickinson*. New York: Simon and Schuster, 1971.

Bird, Isabella. *A Lady's Life in the Rocky Mountains*. New York: G. P. Putnam's Sons, 1883.

Bolton, Sarah K. *Lives of Girls Who Became Famous*. New York: Thomas Y. Crowell Co., 1886.

Davis, Carlyle Channing, and Alderson, William A. *The True Story of Ramona*. New York: Dodge Publishing Co., 1914.

Higgins, David James. *Portrait of Emily Dickinson*. New Brunswick: Rutgers University Press, 1967.

James, George Wharton. *Heroes of California*. Boston: Little, Brown & Co., 1910.

——.*Through Ramona's Country*. Boston: Little, Brown & Co. 1911.

Lummis, Charles F. *The Home of Ramona*. Los Angeles: Charles F. Lummis & Company, n.d.

Moran, Tom, and Sewell, Tom. *Fantasy by the Sea*. Culver City: Peace Press, 1979.

Patterson, Rebecca. *The Riddle of Emily Dickinson*. Boston: Houghton Mifflin, 1951.

Saunders, Charles Francis. *The Story of Carmelita*. Pasadena: A. C. Vroman, 1928.

Taggard, Genevieve. *The Life and Mind of Emily Dickinson*. New York: Alfred A. Knopf, 1930.

Todd, Mabel Loomis, ed. *Letters of Emily Dickinson*. New York: The World Publishing Co., 1951.

Vroman, A. C., and Barnes, T. F. *Ramona's Land*. Los Angeles: Kingsley-Barnes & Neuner Co., 1899.

Walsh, John Evangelist. *The Hidden Life of Emily Dickinson*. New York: Simon and Schuster, 1971.

Wells, Anna Mary. *Dear Preceptor, The Life and Times of Thomas Wentworth Higginson*. Boston: Houghton Mifflin, 1963.

MAGAZINE ARTICLES

Apponyi, Flora Haines. "Last Days of Helen Hunt Jackson." *The Overland Monthly*, September 1885.

Banning, Evelyn. "Helen Hunt Jackson in San Diego." *Journal of San Diego History*, vol. 23, no. 4, Fall 1978.

Battle, Don. "The Man Who Killed Alessandro." *Westways*, February 1962.

Evans, Rosemary. "Helen Hunt Jackson & the Indians." *California Traveler*, August 1969.

Evans, Rosemary. "The Woman." *The California Traveler*, April 1969.

Higginson, Thomas Wentworth. "Mrs. Helen Jackson, 'H. H.'"*Century Magazine*, September 1885.

Kelly, Elizabeth A. "Grandma Varner & 'Tomm.'"*The Overland Monthly*, June 1907.

Marriott, Katheryn E. "Helen Hunt Jackson in Santa Barbara." *Noticias*, vol. XXXXVIIIII, no. 4, Winter 1982.

Marsden, Michael T. "A Dedication to the Memory of Helen Hunt Jackson, 1830–1885." *Arizona and the West,* vol. 21, no. 2, Summer 1979.

Mathes, Valerie Sherer. "Helen Hunt Jackson: Official Agent to the California Mission Indians." *Southern California Quarterly,* vol. LXIII, no. 1, Spring 1981.

Mentor Association staff. "The Last Days of Helen Hunt Jackson." *The Mentor,* vol. 4, no. 21, 1915.

Powell, Lawrence Clark. "California Classics Reread." *Westways,* July 1968.

NEWSPAPER ARTICLES

Los Angeles Express, April 6, 1883.

New York Daily Tribune. "The Starving Utes." February 5, 1880.

New York Independent. "In the White Mountains." September 13, 1866.

New York Independent. April 8, 1880.

New York Independent. "H. H." September 3, 1885.

Oakland Tribune, November 11, 1962.

San Diego Union. March 1, 1882.

San Diego Union. "A Case for Mrs. Helen Hunt Jackson." March 24, 1884.

San Diego Union. "Ramona." March 18, 1887.

San Diego Union. "The Basis of Facts in the Story of 'Ramona' Disclosed." March 20, 1887.

San Diego Union, May 23, 1899.

San Diego Union. Vollie Tripp. "True Story of Ramona Revealed." December 4, 1938.

BOOKS BY HELEN HUNT JACKSON

Bits of Travel. "H. H." Boston: J. R. Osgood and Co., 1870.

Bits of Talk About Home Matters. "H. H." Boston: Roberts Brothers, 1873.

Mercy Philbrick's Choice. The "No Name" Series. Boston: Roberts Brothers, 1876.

Hetty's Strange History. By the author of *Mercy Philbrick's Choice.* Boston: Roberts Brothers, 1877.

Bits of Travel at Home. "H. H." Boston: Roberts Brothers, 1878.

A Century of Dishonor. Helen Hunt Jackson. New York: Harper and Brothers, 1881.

Report on the Conditions and Needs of the Mission Indians. Mrs. Helen Hunt Jackson and Abbot Kinney. Washington, D.C.: Government Printing Office, 1883.

Ramona. Helen Hunt Jackson. Boston: Roberts Brothers, 1884.

MAGAZINE AND NEWSPAPER ARTICLES BY HELEN HUNT JACKSON

New York Evening Post. "The Key to the Casket" (poem) by "Marah." June 7, 1865.

Nation. "Lifted Over" (poem) by "Marah." June 20, 1865.

Nation. "A Burial Service." Unsigned. May 22, 1866.

Century Magazine. "Father Junípero and his Work." "H. H." May 1883.

Century Magazine. "Mission Indians in Southern California, The Present Condition of." "H. H." August 1883.

In addition to the books and periodicals mentioned above, I made use of materials at the Huntington Library, the Special Collections of the Colorado Library, the Pioneer Museum in Colorado Springs, the San Diego Historical Society, the California State Library, and the Milicent Washburn Shinn papers at the California Historical Society.

Index

Abbott, Institute, 8–9, 12, 131
Alcott, Louisa May, 40
Allen, Margaret, 97
Anaheim, 94, 100
Anna and the King of Siam, 28
Apponyi, Flora, 74, 129
Arthur, Chester, 90

Bancroft, H. H., 71
Bandini, Don Juan, 97
Bandini, Ysidora, 97–100, 101
Banfield, Helen 105, 113, 130,
    133–134
Bartlett, Helen, 122–123
Bent, Robert, 66
Bits of Travel, 33
Bits of Travel at Home, 34,
    47, 49
Bright Eyes, 59–60
Brown, John, 23, 134
Brunson & Wells, 101–102,
    111
Byers, William N., 65
Byrnes, M. R, 86

Carr, Ezra, 84–85
Carr, Jeanne, 84–86, 127–8

Castillo, Jesus (Captain), 80,
    82, 83, 90, 100,
    113–114, 131
Cate, Dr. Hamiltan J., 40, 83,
    113, 130
Century, 69, 70, 75–76, 87,
    92, 129
Century of Dishonor, 2,
    62–64, 89, 96, 102,
    131–132
Chivington, Col. J. M., 64, 66
Christian Union, 112, 121
Cleveland, Grover, 132
Closa, Valentine, 87
Colfax, 35
Cooper, Ellwood, 75
Coronel, Don Antonia,
    73–74–75, 86, 106,
    120–121, 124–125
Coronel, Dona Mariana,
    73–74, 86, 106,
    120–121, 124–125
Couts, Cave, 97–98
Couts, Cave, Jr., 99–100, 107,
    109

Davis, Carlyle C., 66
Dawes Act, 136

del Rio, Dolores, 136
Denver News, 65
Dickinson, Emily, 6, 7, 8, 14, 19, 26, 40, 44, 45, 53, 55, 56, 116, 117, 123, 133
Dickinson, Lavinia, 55, 57
Diego, Juan, 98, 99, 107, 135
Diego, Ramona, 98, 99

El Recreo, 73, 120
Emerson, Ralph Waldo, 1, 25, 89, 134
Estudillo family, 78, 80, 89, 97
Estudillo residence 78, 89

Fages, Pedro, 71
Federal Bureau of Indian Affairs, 56
Field, Kate, 90
Fields, James, Thomas, 26–27
Fiske, Ann, 2–3, 7, 14, 21, 44, 105
Deborah Fiske, 3–7
Nathan Fiske, 3–7

Gilder, Jeanette and Joseph, 67, 103
Gilder, Richard Watson, 69, 92–93
Gish, Lillian, 136
Glimpses of California and the Missions, 93
Golden Gate Bay, 37
Godwin, Parke, 22, 23

Harper's Monthly, 68
Hartford Courant, 39, 68
Hemet, 136

Hetty's Strange History, 58
H. H., 23, 28, 33, 54, 77, 113, 118, 120
Higginson, Mary, 24, 28–29, 44, 51–52
Higginson, Thomas Wentworth, 23–31, 39, 40, 44, 51, 52, 53, 55, 61–62, 64, 93, 104, 107–110, 134
Holm, Saxe, 29, 33, 54, 69
Holmes, Oliver Wendell, 58
Howe, Julia Ward, 25
Horton, Alonzo, 76
Horton House, 76
Hunt, Edward Bissel, 11–20, 53
Hunt, Murray, 16–17
Hunt, Warren Horsford (Rennie), 17–22, 77, 107
Hunter Cats of Connorloa, 116

Interior Department, 65, 72, 93
Indian Rights Association, 125, 136

Jackson, Helen Hunt,
birth of, 3
development as a writer, 22–27
as a U. S. Commissioner, 89–96, 100–103
marriage to Edward Hunt, 15
marriage to William Jackson, 44
death of, 132
Jackson, William Sharpless, 1, 42–46, 49–52, 56–58, 68–69, 72, 87–90, 93, 102, 105–106, 111, 113–115, 119, 122–125, 129–132

Jolon, 87
Jary, Victor, 136
Journalist, 122–124

Kimball Mansion, 83, 86, 100, 110
King and I, 28
Kinney, Abbot, 83, 86–87, 90–95, 100–102, 110–111, 134
Kinneyloa, 86, 116, 120

La Jolla Indians, 99
Lawson, S. S., 100
Leonowens, Anna, 27–28
Little Women, 40
Longfellow, Henry Wadsworth, 52
Long Beach, 98, 124
Los Angeles, 73, 83, 84, 86, 88, 100, 102, 116, 117, 120, 129, 134
Los Angeles Express, 96

Masque of Poets, 54–57
Mercy Philbrick's Choice, 50
Milwaukee Sentinel, 123
Mission San Antonio de Padua, 87, 103
Mission Santa Barbara, 71, 75
Mitchell, Newell, 94–96, 100
Morse, Emphraim, 77, 107
Muir, John, 127–8, 133

Napa Valley, 37
Nation, 28, 33
New York Evening Post, 22
New York Herald, 8

New York Independent, 44–45, 84, 91, 93, 103, 113
New York Tribune, 65
Niles, Thomas, 132
"No Name" Series, 51, 54, 56, 58

Overland Monthly, 48, 75

Pala Indians, 99, 107
Palmer, Julius, 9, 12, 13, 14
Palmer, Ray, 9, 12–13, 15
Palmer, Mrs. Ray, 13–17
Pasadena, 84
Pico, Pio, 72
Point Loma, 77
Ponca Indians, 59, 60–61, 66
Price, Hiram, 90–91, 103
Publisher's Weekly, 121

Ramona, 2–3, 78, 82, 85–86, 94–95, 112, 114, 121–123, 131-133, 135–136
Ramona Pageant, 136
Rancho Camulos, 109
Rancho Guajome, 100, 109
Riverside, 84, 102, 136
Robert's Brothers, 51, 56, 57, 92, 121, 131
Rocky Mountain News, 44, 65

Saboba, 80, 89, 90, 100–101, 111–112, 114
Sacramento, 36
San Bernardino, 82, 84, 98, 102
Sandham, Henry, 86, 87, 94, 95, 100

Sand Hill Massacre, 64–66
San Diego, 76, 78, 79, 84, 86,
    96, 97, 107, 117, 120,
    122, 136
San Diego Union, 76, 133, 136
San Francisco, 36, 79, 83, 87,
    124, 125, 127, 129
San Francisco Chronicle, 77
San Gabriel Mountains, 84, 85
San Gabriel Valley, 102, 111
San Jacinto Valley, 80, 81
San Jose, 37
San Juan Capistrano, 86
San Juan Bautista, 87
San Luis Rey Indians, 79, 86,
    107
San Pasquale Reservation, 79,
    111
San Pedro, 98
Santa Barbara, 75, 76, 84, 86,
    109
Santa Clara Valley, 37
Santa Cruz, 37
San Ysidro Valley Indians, 94
Schurz, Carl, 2, 62, 72
Scribner's, 33
Secularization Act, 74
Serra, Father Junipero, 70–72
Serrano Indians, 80
Sheriff, Mary, 80–83, 89,
    100–101, 103, 107,
    111, 131
Standing Bear, 59–60
Stearns, Don Abel, 98
Stone, Lucy, 27
Stowe, Harriet Beecher, 16, 40,
    108, 122

Teller, Henry, 89, 90–91, 111
Temecula, 79, 106, 107, 111
Temecula Indians, 111
Temple, Sam, 98, 107, 135
Thacher, Mary Potter, 52–53
Training of Children, 92
True Story of Ramona, 66
Two Years Before the Mast, 97

Ubach, Father Anthony,
    77–80
Uncle Tom's Cabin, 3, 16, 67,
    122

Venice, 84, 135
Vista, 97

Ward, William Hayes, 44–45,
    50, 84, 108, 113
Warner, Charles Dudley, 68,
    91
Welch, Raquel, 136
Whipple, Mrs. E. W., 96–97,
    117, 119, 120, 124
Woolsey, Sarah, 32–33, 35,
    37, 131
Wynkoop, E. W., 64–66

Yosemite, 37, 127
Young, Loretta, 136

Zeph, 132

Other titles in Chronicle Books
Literary West series:

Mark Twain in California
by Nigey Lennon

Robert Louis Stevenson in California
by Roy Nickerson

John Steinbeck: The California Years
by Brian St. Pierre

Ambrose Bierce: The Making of a Misanthrope
by Richard Saunders

Robinson Jeffers: Poet of California
by James Karman

PLATE 1 *Helen Fiske following her graduation from the Abbott Institute*

PLATE 3 *William Sharpless Jackson was a man who knew what he wanted*

PLATE 2 *Lieutenant Edward Hunt soon after his marriage to Helen Fiske*

PLATE 4 *Helen chose the Camulos Ranch as the setting for much of* Ramona

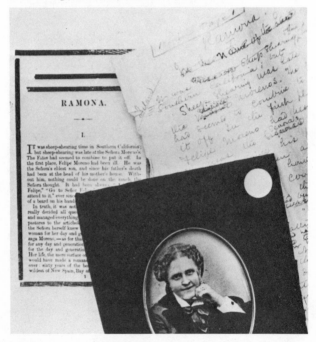

PLATE 5 *The original* Ramona *manuscript*

PLATE 6 (Right) *Ramona as one artist imagined her*

PLATE 7 *Indian women washing their linen as "Ramona" did*

PLATE 8 *Ramona and Alessandro might have lived in this typical Indian dwelling of the 1880s*

PLATE 9 (Right) *A real Indian woman of Ramona's time*

PLATE 10 *Loretta Young and Don Ameche
as Ramona and Alessandro in the
20th Century-Fox production*